on track ...

Genesis

every album, every song

Stuart Macfarlane

sonicbondpublishing.com

Sonicbond Publishing Limited
www.sonicbondpublishing.co.uk
Email: info@sonicbondpublishing.co.uk

First Published in the United Kingdom 2019
First Published in the United States 2019

British Library Cataloguing in Publication Data:
A Catalogue record for this book is available from the British Library

Copyright Stuart Macfarlane 2019

ISBN 978-1-78952-005-7

Typset in ITC Garamond & Berthold Akzidenz Grotesk
Printed and bound in England

Graphic design and typesetting: Full Moon Media

Dedication

This book is dedicated to my father, Donald Macfarlane,
a quiet, hard-working family man who introduced me to
music at an early age and was the best role model anyone
could wish for.

Acknowledgements

Love and thanks to my wife Caroline for her enthusiasm and
encouragement, but mostly her patience and understanding
during the long hours spent writing this book. Who knew it
would take so much time to write a wee book?

To Iain Brown, John Wootton and Graeme McNaught, my
Genesis gig buddies over the years, thanks for helping
create great and lasting memories.

Thanks to the many Genesis internet fan sites who continue
to provide a wealth of information online and have been
invaluable in validating details.

To Stephen Lambe at Sonicbond Publishing, a friend for
many years who helped push me in the nicest possible
way into writing this. Thanks for the opportunity,
encouragement and the help throughout the process of
creating this book.

Thanks to Catherine Smith, the archivist at Charterhouse for
providing access to the school's online archive.

Finally, thanks to Tony Banks, Mike Rutherford, Phil
Collins, Steve Hackett, Peter Gabriel, Anthony Phillips, Ray
Wilson, John Mayhew, John Silver and Chris Stewart for the
wonderful legacy of music you created, without which my
teenage years would have been missing something special,
and this book would not exist.

on track ...
Genesis

Contents

Band Members

Tony Banks (born 27 March 1950)
Keyboards, guitars, backing vocals
1967-Present
Anthony George Banks was born in East Sussex, the youngest of five children.
He started learning the piano at the age of eight. He met Peter Gabriel when
they both started at Charterhouse, became best friends and formed their early
band The Garden Wall together. Once described by manager Tony Smith as 'the
only irreplaceable member of Genesis', he has performed on every Genesis
release. His classical training has helped his playing and writing, but it is his
distinctive melodic style and in particular, his piano skills for which he is most
noted. Banks has released solo material under his own name and using the
band name Bankstatement. He has scored movie soundtracks and written
classical music but has enjoyed limited success compared with the other
members of the band. Since the 2007 world tour, he has recorded two more
orchestral releases, *Six Pieces for Orchestra* in 2012 and the excellent *Five* in
2018.

Mike Rutherford (born 2 October 1950)
Bass, guitars, backing vocals
1967-Present
Born Michael John Cloete Crawford Rutherford in Portsmouth, England, Mike
was given his first guitar at the age of eight and appeared in his first band, The
Chesters, the following year. An original member of Genesis, he has played
on every Genesis album, taking over lead guitar duties when Steve Hackett
left the band in 1977. Best known for his custom Rickenbacker and Shergold
double neck guitars, and for his use of bass pedals, Rutherford has also had a
successful solo career with his other band Mike and The Mechanics, topping
the charts in 1988 with the single 'Living Years'.

Peter Gabriel (born 13 February 1950)
Vocals, Flute
1967-1975
Born Peter Brian Gabriel in Chobham, Surrey, Genesis' shy and enigmatic
vocalist and frontman met Banks as they entered Charterhouse school in
1963, becoming best friends with the pianist. Through their early musical
experiments, they formed the group The Garden Wall which would later
expand into Genesis. Often seen as flamboyant – though much of this was
to help deal with his extreme shyness – his unique vocal style, between-song
story-telling and 'dressing up' in the band's early days attracted strong media
attention, helping to promote and build an audience for the group. After
leaving in 1975, Gabriel built a successful solo career, his album *So* achieving

triple platinum in the UK and quintuple platinum in the US. His love of both new technology and world musical styles are groundbreaking, while the video for 'Sledgehammer' has been shown more than any other on rock video station MTV. He was asked to write the music for the show *OVO* which was performed multiple times per day in the centre of the Millennium Dome in London throughout the year 2000. Like Phil Collins, he has received a string of awards and accolades during his career, including three Brit awards, six Grammys, thirteen MTV awards and the Ivor Novello award for Lifetime Achievement. Having been inducted into the Rock and Roll hall of fame with Genesis in 2010, he was also inducted for his solo work in 2014. An active and outspoken human rights champion, he has worked closely with Amnesty International, helped set up organisations such as WITNESS and 'The Elders' and is described as one of Rock's most political musicians by AllMusic. His 'Real World' studios in Box, Wiltshire has become something of a mecca for musicians and fans, used by artists of all genres, as diverse as Tom Jones, Robert Plant, Amy Winehouse and Kanye West.

Anthony Phillips (born 23 December 1951)
Guitars
1967-1970
Born Anthony Edwin Phillips in Roehampton, London, he was the youngest, but most experienced and accomplished of the early Genesis members, writing his first song at age thirteen on his newly acquired Fender Stratocaster. He first met Rutherford, then later Gabriel and Banks, while at Charterhouse school. His contribution to the early band was considerable, and his influence on the twelve-string guitar style of the band was felt for many years after his departure. Philips featured on *From Genesis To Revelation* and *Trespass* and played his last gig with Genesis at Haywards Heath in Sussex on 18 July 1970. After leaving the band, it would be seven years before he would release his first solo album *The Geese And The Ghost*. Phillips has played keyboards and guitar on several projects, including early demos for Peter Gabriel, Rutherford's 1980 solo project *Smallcreep's Day* and Camel's 1982 release *The Single Factor*. Since 1977 he has been the most prolific of any member of Genesis, releasing 33 fully-fledged albums and twelve collections of pieces.

Phil Collins (born 30 January 1951)
Drums, Vocals
August 1970 – March 1996, 2007
Philip David Charles Collins was born in London and started playing the drums from the age of five, going to drama school at fourteen. On joining Genesis, he immediately lifted and tightened the sound, forging a solid rhythmic backbone with Rutherford. His skills as an arranger were used regularly to absorb the ideas of others and build on them. His reluctant decision to sing on *A Trick of the Tail* after Gabriel's departure would also prove to be a catalyst for a

very successful solo career. As a solo artist, he generated even more hits than he did with Genesis, with seven US number one singles and six UK number one albums. Solo and as a part of Genesis, he has also sold over 150 million albums making him one of only three musicians who has sold over 100 million records as a band and as a solo artist, the others being Michael Jackson and Paul McCartney. Given how the purchasing patterns of music have changed, it is unlikely anyone else will achieve this feat. During the 1980s, he had more US top 40 hits than any other artist. The list of credits and awards are long; indeed, it is sometimes hard to believe they were all achieved by one person. He has won eight Grammy awards, six Brits, two Golden Globes, an Oscar, and six Ivor Novello's. A Phil Collins 'star' was added on the Hollywood Walk of fame in 1999, and he was inducted into the Songwriters Hall of Fame in 2003, the Rock and Roll hall of fame with Genesis in 2010, the Modern Drummer Hall of Fame in 2012 and the Classic Drummer Hall of Fame in 2013. Collins undertook his *Not Dead Yet* world tour of his solo material in 2018-2019 with his son Nicholas on drums. At the time of writing, he is no longer able to play the drums for any length of time, and after back surgery, must walk with a stick due to the loss of feeling in one foot.

Steve Hackett (born 12 February 1950)
Guitars
January 1971 – October 1977
Born Steven Richard Hackett in Pimlico, London, Steve didn't start playing the guitar until he was twelve years old. Though he has never had any formal tuition, his unique style of playing, particularly his use of the volume pedal, is a trademark of early Genesis and would continue to influence the sound of the band after his departure. Of all the members of the band except Phillips, Hackett has been the most prolific, releasing 25 studio albums, including *At The Edge Of Light* in 2019. In 1996 he released *Genesis Revisited*, a set of reworkings of classic Genesis songs, and added another collection in 2012. Following these two albums, he has toured extensively playing Genesis-orientated sets. 2019 saw him touring North America and Europe playing all of *Selling England by the Pound* and celebrating 40 years since the release of his 1979 solo album *Spectral Mornings*.

Ray Wilson (born 8 September 1968)
Vocals
1996-1998
Raymond Wilson from Dumfries, Scotland was lead singer with Stiltskin, who's single 'Inside' reached number one in the UK charts in 1994. Wilson took over vocal duties from Collins in 1996 and recorded one album with the band, *Calling All Stations*. Since the band went on indefinite hiatus, Wilson has carried on with his solo career, releasing six studio and nine live albums. He has recorded and appeared live with Hackett performing Genesis material.

John Silver (born 1950)

Drums
1968 – August 1969
Jonathan Silver played on *From Genesis To Revelation* apart from 'Silent Sun',
then left shortly after the release to study leisure management at Cornell
University in the US.

John Mayhew (born 27 March 1947, died 26 March 2009)

Drums
August 1969 – August 1970
Having played on *Trespass*, little is known of Mayhew's whereabouts until
2006 when he turned up at a Genesis convention. He died in Glasgow in 2009,
where he was working as a carpenter for a manufacturer of furniture.

Chris Stewart (born 1950)

Drums
1967-1968
Stewart joined Gabriel and Banks in The Garden Wall in 1967. He played on
the first two singles 'Silent Sun' and 'Winter's Tale' and is credited on *From
Genesis To Revelation* for 'Silent Sun'. Having left the band at the request
of Jonathan King, he later moved to Spain to be a sheep shearer on a farm.
Stewart is also a successful writer, publishing a trilogy of books about his
exploits. *Driving Over Lemons: An Optimist in Andalucia*, the first book, sold
over one million copies and has been translated into nine languages.

Mick Barnard

Guitar
October 1970 – January 1971
Barnard joined Genesis several months after Philips left, and played with the
band for only three months before Hackett joined. During that time he played
30 gigs with the band and helped develop the guitar parts for the *Nursery
Cryme* album. He went on to have a successful career in Audio Engineering,
founding the Bel Digital Audio company.

Introduction and a brief history

The first Genesis album *From Genesis to Revelation* was released on 7 March 1969. During this time the band have undergone several changes in personnel and musical direction and have released fifteen studio and six live albums. They have achieved album sales of more than 150 million, playing their last gig in front of over half a million fans at the Circus Maximus in Rome in 2007, and were inducted into the Rock and Roll Hall of Fame in 2010. There is no doubt that albums such as *The Lamb Lies Down On Broadway*, *Foxtrot* and *Selling England By The Pound* played a huge part in helping to define progressive rock and are considered classics of the genre. The band are even more widely recognised for the later period of their career as a hugely successful rock and pop band with a string of top ten hits on both sides of the Atlantic, including five number one albums in a row in the UK. While the band enjoyed some limited earlier success with 'Your Own Special Way' and 'Follow You Follow Me', in the 1970s, it was singles like 'I Can't Dance', 'Land Of Confusion' and the US number one 'Invisible Touch', that made the band a household name throughout the world.

The original four members of Genesis met while they were at Charterhouse, a boys-only boarding school near Godalming, Surrey, England where Lord Baden-Powell, the founder of the scout movement, had attended almost 100 years earlier. Peter Gabriel and Tony Banks were already good friends, having met when they entered the school in 1963. As a duo, they played the pop music hits of the time, including songs by the Beatles and soul singers like Otis Redding, who was a favourite of Gabriel. With Banks on Piano and Gabriel on vocals and flute, they formed a band, calling themselves The Garden Wall. Both were friends with Anthony Phillips who was playing in a band called 'The Anon' with Michael Rutherford. The Garden Wall played their first gig at Charterhouse one afternoon in July 1966 at an event organised by Richard MacPhail, then the singer with The Anon. MacPhail would later take up a role as a roadie, sound engineer and tour manager for Genesis and, later, with Peter Gabriel. That particular show had The Garden Wall playing second, with The Anon headlining, but having no drummer other than Gabriel, who couldn't sing and play at the same time, The Garden Wall brought in Chris Stewart on drums and convinced Rivers Job and Phillips from The Anon to join them on bass and guitar respectively.

To fully understand the significance of this gig, we need to recognise that single-sex boarding schools were no easy rich boys' playground, and like many of the public schools in England, Charterhouse created a strict environment intended to focus minds on learning and personal development in traditional directions. The atmosphere was, by design, oppressive with little flexibility or tolerance for anything that deviated from the curriculum or could in the slightest way appear to discredit the school. Modern music was thus considered pretty much the work of the devil, with pop stars such as Mick Jagger viewed as if they were the antichrist. Rutherford was banned from golf to focus more on team sports and later prevented from playing the guitar as it was seen as 'the instrument of the revolution', though he firmly believes it just made him more determined to play. It was, therefore, with some trepidation that music master Geoffrey Ford agreed to allow the concert to take place at the school. It was arranged for the last afternoon of the term, leaving the whole of the long summer holiday period to diffuse any dissent or disruptive behaviour it might create. A further indication of the sensitivity of such an event was that Ford had specified that no announcements should be made from the stage. During The Anon set, MacPhail spoke to fill in during a technical issue, and Ford stopped the gig after their next song, saying that MacPhail had 'defied him'. The school magazine, The Carthusian, is a quarterly publication, covering every sporting encounter, school leaver and classical concert at the school, but fails to mention the event. However, one article does appear in the November 1966 edition, titled 'Why Not Pop' and covers the bands that had formed at the school, including The Anon, The Garden Wall, The Scarlet and Black and The Climax, which also featured Rutherford on rhythm guitar.

Banks and Gabriel were starting to write some of their own songs when they heard that Phillips and Rutherford were looking to make a tape. Banks offered to help if his band could record a song too. During the Easter holidays of 1967, the four recorded one song from Banks and Gabriel and five songs from Phillips and Rutherford. Two tracks from that tape would feature on the first album in different forms. 'She Is Beautiful' by Gabriel and Banks would receive new lyrics and be renamed 'The Serpent', and the instrumental 'Patricia' from Phillips and Rutherford would have lyrics added and become 'In Hiding'. A friend of the band passed a copy of the tape to Jonathan King with a note saying, 'these are Charterhouse boys, have a listen'. King, who had a hit single in 1965 with his own composition, 'Everyone's Gone To The Moon', reaching four in the UK charts and seventeen in the USA was an old boy of Charterhouse and was visiting for a former pupil's event. King was impressed enough, particularly by Gabriel's interesting voice, to fund a series of recording sessions for the band producing their first single, 'Silent Sun', which was released on 22 February 1968 on the Decca label. It was just before the release of the single that King gave the band the name Genesis, as the group had declined to adopt his initial suggestion – 'Gabriel's Angels'.

King also produced the first album *From Genesis To Revelation*, which was released in March 1969 to little acclaim, selling only around 600 copies. At the time of recording the album, Genesis consisted of Peter Gabriel on vocals and flute, Tony Banks on keyboards, Mike Rutherford on bass and guitars, Anthony Phillips on guitars and John Silver on drums, who had replaced Chris Stewart. Phillips was already determined to develop a career in music; Rutherford was planning to go to Edinburgh University to study English, Banks was already at university in Sussex studying chemistry and Gabriel was planning to go to film school after that summer. They continued to work on material during the summer holidays at various houses of family and friends, and by the end of the Summer, the band had decided to make a go of it, with Phillips having convinced Rutherford, while Banks and Gabriel eventually convinced each other. Banks decided to take a year out of university, seeing this as a once in a lifetime opportunity while his parents thought that he would get it out of his system in that year. However, by this point King and Decca had lost interest, allowing the band to move on as free agents.

Trespass was to follow in 1970 with John Mayhew replacing John Silver on drums. While the album did not chart in the UK or US, it reached number one in Belgium, with the band attracting a small but growing cult following, drawn to the longer, increasingly complex musical arrangements, and the nervous storytelling and early stage presence of Gabriel. Around this time Phillips decided to leave the band as he was suffering severe stage fright and had been advised by his doctor to quit the band following a bout of bronchial pneumonia. By 1971 Phil Collins had replaced John Mayhew on drums, and Steve Hackett had taken over from Phillips on guitars, after a short stint by Mick Barnard. Over the next three years, the release of *Nursery Cryme*, *Foxtrot* and *Selling England by the Pound* positioned Genesis as one of the top progressive rock bands of the era. When *The Lamb Lies Down On Broadway* was released in 1975 it was to mark the end of the Gabriel era with their most ambitious album to date.

The departure of Gabriel led to significant doubt as to whether the band could go on and Collins even proposed they consider continuing as an instrumental group. This era was to be the start of the rise of Phil Collins, first as a front man for Genesis, then later with the start of a hugely successful solo career. It would see Genesis move from cult, almost underground, status to become a major international rock band. *A Trick of the Tail* and *Wind and Wuthering* were both released in 1976, the first time this author saw the band live. Hackett would leave the band in 1977, just days before the release of their superb live album *Seconds Out*. Once again, the band decided to continue, this time as a three piece with Rutherford taking over the guitar parts in the studio. *...and then there were three...* being the result in 1978.

The next phase of the band's career came with the release of *Duke* in 1980 and *Abacab* in 1981. By the time *Genesis* was released in 1983 and *Invisible Touch* three years later, they were regularly playing stadiums and festivals and enjoying significant commercial success in both the album and singles charts. After another gap of five years, *We Can't Dance* was released, with the band playing to 90,000 people at the Knebworth festival in the UK – one of my most memorable live experiences.

In March 1996, after five years without a new studio album, and three years since their last live show, Collins departed to focus on his solo career, at which point most fans felt that it was finally over for the band. However in 1997, to everyone's surprise, *Calling All Stations* was released with Ray Wilson on lead vocals. This was to be the last studio release from the band to date. Rumours of, and excitement at, a reunion tour with Hackett and Gabriel to perform *The*

Lamb Lies Down on Broadway quickly subsided as an agreement to proceed became hard to achieve. Eventually, the continuing dialogue between band members became the *Turn It On Again: The Tour* of 2007 with Collins, Banks and Rutherford and familiar cohorts Daryl Stuermer on guitars and Chester Thompson on drums. The concert CD *Live Over Europe 2007* and DVD *When In Rome* were recorded on the last performance of the European tour in front of an estimated audience of 500,000, making it one of the largest concerts ever staged.

When the BBC documentary *Together and Apart* aired on 4 October 2014, rumours of another reunion were high. However, while the band members have not ruled it out, the possibility seems to be becoming increasingly remote. Despite having to use a walking stick after back surgery and no longer able to play the drums, Collins set out on his *Not Dead Yet* world tour in June 2017, playing 81 dates over two years. In late 2018, he said a reunion is still possible if his son Nicholas, who was touring with him, played the drums.

This book will take you through a more detailed history of Genesis, covering each album in turn and examining every track. It details events during and between each recording and captures the impact the band had on its fans, and in particular, the author. It has required revisiting their entire catalogue of work, bringing back many great memories, and it is hoped that the book will do the same for long term fans, as well as providing some deeper context and insight for newer fans of the band. I have tried wherever possible to verify the details, but if you find any inaccuracies and omissions, please contact the publishers so they can be corrected in a future edition.

From Genesis to Revelation (1969)

Personnel:
Peter Gabriel: lead vocals, flute
Tony Banks: organ, piano, backing vocals
Anthony Phillips: guitars, backing vocals
Mike Rutherford: bass guitar, guitar, backing vocals
John Silver: drums (except on 'Silent Sun')
Chris Stewart: drums on 'Silent Sun'
Recorded at Regent Sound studio in London in August 1968
Producer: Jonathan King
Sleeve design from an idea by Jonathan King
Released: March 7 1969
Label: Decca/London Records
Highest Chart places: UK: Did not chart, US: Did not chart
Running time: 43:25

While *Trespass* is often considered the first 'real' Genesis release, even by some of the band themselves, *From Genesis To Revelation* remains overlooked. Rutherford would later call it 'a bunch of kids on holiday time' and refers to *Trespass* as the first album from Genesis as a band. However, Banks is more philosophical, saying:

> *I have quite a lot of affection for **From Genesis To Revelation**. I don't love it or anything, but it was part of my childhood.*

It did, however, play an important part in their development, and as 'every album, every track' means just that, let's go back over 50 years and start there.

While From Genesis To Revelation was released in 1969, most of the tracks had been written between 1967 and 1968 with demos recorded at several sessions arranged by Jonathan King. Two singles were released in advance of the album, 'The Silent Sun' with 'That's Me' as the B-Side on 22 February 1968 and 'A Winter's Tale' with 'One Eyed Hound' as the B-Side on 10 May 1968. Sales were nothing special, but it was enough to convince King and Decca to invest further in a full album. For some reason, 'A Winter Tale' was never included on the original release, even though it was stronger than many of the songs that made it to the final album. At the time, the band viewed themselves primarily as songwriters and had focused on 'straight pop songs,' as Rutherford later called them, in the hope that others would record them. As was the case with many artists at the time, without at least some chart success it was difficult to start out as a songwriter, so recording your own material yourself was often a better option. Indeed, Elton John says the only reason he started to record his songs was that he and Bernie Taupin, couldn't find anyone to record them.

Written against a backdrop of the chart success of late sixties psychedelia, the album itself is consistent with the tone of many contemporary bands, a time when The Beatles, Donovan, The Kinks, The Who and occasionally even Pink Floyd were regularly in the top 10 in the UK. The Bee Gees had reached number one with their first single 'Massachusetts' in 1967, definitely, an influence on some of the songs that Genesis were writing, while the first single 'The Silent Sun', was written to appease King who wanted them to simplify their arrangements for commercial reasons.

The band were daunted at the prospect of filling a whole 'Long Player', so King proposed a concept album loosely based on the Bible's 'Book of Genesis' with short instrumental pieces linking the songs. Rutherford claims they were too young and insecure to tell King to 'piss off' with his suggestion. In the inter-song links, we hear many short piano and guitar pieces with chord progressions and textures that hint at what would come later. The concept itself isn't strictly adhered to throughout the album, with only a few songs lyrically portraying the 'Book of Genesis' such as 'In The Beginning', 'Fireside Song' and 'The Serpent', but several take a more abstract slant on the concept. In the Bible, 'Genesis' covers the creation of Earth in six days, the story of Adam and Eve, Noah's ark and the destruction of Sodom and Gomorrah, through to the rise of the Israelites and the story of Joseph, later to be immortalised in Rice and Lloyd Webber's famous musical.'

While all the tracks are credited to Genesis, the band were still writing in pairs. Rutherford concedes that he and Phillips hadn't progressed with their songwriting as much as Gabriel and Banks, who wrote most of the album. It was recorded in just three days in August 1968 at Regent Sound studio B in Denmark Street, just off Charing Cross Road in London. Strings were later added to some of the tracks, as was common at the time, but was something that the band were not initially aware of, and strongly disagreed with, causing Phillips to storm out of the studio on the last day of mixing.

King had come up with the name Genesis, to signify that it was early in his production career as much as anything else, but it was discovered relatively late that the name was already in use by a band in the US. King refused to change it, coming up with the idea of having a black album sleeve with the title in small gothic characters, so as not to feature the band name. Of course, this did little to promote the album visually in the racks of the record stores. Records were often purchased after a lengthy browse through the sleeves in a store, and in many cases, the initial impact of the sleeve design had as much to do with a potential purchase as the band name or their music. Having no information on the back of the cover meant it was often classified as religious music based on the title and was filed under that section in stores. That the band chose to be known as Genesis in the UK and Revelation internationally, a name that thankfully didn't last long, didn't help much. King now accepts that all of this was a bad idea and probably hindered the band's success. But what if the album had been a success? Would the band's reinvention as a progressive rock band have been hindered 50 years ago?

The album sold between 600 and 700 copies in the following year. The album does contain several strong songs that could have been hits given the right promotion, such as 'In The Wilderness' and 'Silent Sun'. Certainly, the sleeve design and the unfortunate religious classification were factors, but Decca also lacked experience in promoting a band who were somewhat out of the ordinary. King was also losing interest after the release of the album and was not eager to follow the band towards the more experimental and complex direction in which they were heading. Due to the diligence of their parents, given how young the boys were at the time, the proposed five-year deal was reduced to one year and the band parted company with both King and Decca in late 1969.

King still retains the rights and associated recordings under the JonJo publishing name and has released it under several titles, often adding additional tracks from the early demo recordings. At the time of writing, at least ten different versions of the album have been released, under various names including *In the Beginning, Rock Roots, Where the Sour Turns to Sweet, And the Word Was* and *Genesis*. Tapes of some additional material recorded at the time were found in storage at Regent Sound Studios when the studio was sold, and a collection of these and some new mixes were released as a digital download in 2017 titled *Genesis 50 Years Ago*. The tag line: 'Featuring recently discovered multi-tracks never heard before' was used on the cover although, this being 1968, the songs were only recorded in four tracks anyway, with the band on track one, vocals on track two and (usually) strings and brass on the other two tracks. Banks notes that the band did try to recover the rights, but that King wanted a substantial sum in return.

'Where the Sour Turns to Sweet' 3:14 (Genesis)
Originally planned to be the first single, but shelved after things didn't work out in the studio, this song demonstrates the band's early ability to write short songs with multiple parts and tempo changes. However, the use of finger snaps – very much a pop cliché from the era – is one of the many things which date the song. Strings and brass were added later before the album was released. This song was eventually released as the third single, the first after the release of the album, in June 1969 with 'In Hiding' as the B-side.

'In the Beginning' 3:42 (Genesis)
This is a song about the Genesis of the Earth but could as well be about the band itself with its hook line, 'it has begun, you're are in the hands of destiny'. The seas, land and mountains are violently formed and 'life is on its way'. The track is one of the few songs that reflect the concept of the album lyrically. The song starts with a single tone oscillation which must have seemed very modern at the time, and there are several layers of acoustic guitars which bury the piano in the background. Banks brings the song to a close with a nice chord progression on piano.

'Fireside Song' 4:16 (Genesis)

The intro to this song features Banks on piano again, with a chord progression that hints at the style of many future pieces he would write with Genesis. The rest of the song is an airy vocal and acoustic guitar number with the addition of strings, following on the story of creation with the appearance of flora and fauna. It is one of the better pieces on the album, with a decent folk-style chorus reminiscent of Donovan and some of the other folk artists of the day.

'The Serpent' 4:36 (Genesis)

'The Serpent' is one of only two tracks from the original six-song demo tape made in 1967 to have found its way onto the album, the other being 'In Hiding'. Originally titled 'She is Beautiful', it was the only Banks and Gabriel song to be recorded on that demo tape. With a different title and lyrics, it is another of the songs to follow the concept via the lines ', and God created man from dust. With a soul inside his mould. And God created womankind. The vessel of Satan's hold'. This song could easily have held its own against many other 'hits' of the time with a powerful baseline and strong psychedelic vibe.

'Am I Very Wrong?' 3:28 (Genesis)

After another 40 seconds of piano from Banks, acoustic guitars, flute and Gabriel's vocals combine in a song with a verse that is closer to *Trespass* than any other on the first album. The simple chorus seems to exist to commercialise the song, and it sounds like Rutherford singing it.

'In the Wilderness' 3:21 (Genesis)

'In the Wilderness' is the most commercial song on the album, with a very catchy chorus, although for some reason it was never released as a single. In its verse, Gabriel shows signs of the vocal style he would pioneer on later albums with the way he annunciates the lyrics and a slightly hoarse, strained tone in his voice.

'Conqueror' 3:44 (Genesis)

The song starts with a reprise of 'In The Wilderness' on tremolo guitar. 'Conqueror' is in the style of Bob Dylan, also suggesting the vocal styling of Liam Gallagher of Oasis (indeed, this is the only Genesis album he claims to like) with the extended syllable at the end of each line of the chorus.

'In Hiding' 2:56 (Genesis)

This is another track that was given strings in post-production, though you would be forgiven for thinking it was a Mellotron used on the song. It was originally recorded on their first demo tape in 1967 as an instrumental titled 'Patricia', and that version would be released later on some of the many later versions of this album as well as on the *Genesis Archive 1967-1975* collection. The song was also issued as the B-side to 'When The Sour Turns To Sweet' in June 1969.

'One Day' 3:16 (Genesis)

Apart from Gabriel's vocal and some strummed guitar, little remains of the other instruments on this track beyond the intro, buried as they are under a heavy orchestral arrangement. It is easy to understand why Phillips, in particular, was so angry at the addition of the strings. Overall, it is another easy-going, commercial track that might have been released as single.

'Window' 3:53 (Genesis)

A short piano introduction – mistakes and all – is played as the link to this track and acoustic guitar, strings and horns form the backing to this endearing, quirky love song.

'In Limbo' 3:06 (Genesis)

After a rather pointless instrumental introduction that adds nothing to the song, 'In Limbo' kicks in with a 'flower power' vibe, as Gabriel sings 'take me away to the furthest star in the sky'. It has a similar, joyful feel to 'I Can't Let Maggie Go' by Honeybus, used in a famous UK advert for Nimble low-calorie bread in the 1970s.

'The Silent Sun' 2:08 (Genesis)

The second single from the band, and the first from the album, 'The Silent Sun' was released in February 1968 in advance of the album launch with 'That's Me' as the B-side. Gabriel's vocals more than suggest the Bee Gees, with multipart harmonies in the chorus. A remastered single version would be released under the name Peter Gabriel and Genesis in 2006 with 'When The Sour Turns To Sweet' as the B-Side.

'A Place to Call My Own' 1:57 (Genesis)

A rather more sombre, but delightfully simple track ends the album, featuring vocal and piano, but with a melody and vocal delivery that wouldn't be out of place on *The Lamb Lies Down On Broadway*. The second part of the song has more orchestration than is needed, once again.

Related Tracks

While there are many early demo tracks now available, few add much to the story of the band and have not been included here. There are three pieces, however, that are particularly worthy of note.

'Patricia' 3:05 (Genesis)

Patricia is an instrumental from the original demo tape recorded at Easter 1967 that was given to Jonathan King. This is the only track from that original recording that has been released and as expected the quality isn't great, but this is notable as the earliest available recording of the original four young members of the band, Banks (sixteen years old), Gabriel (seventeen), Phillips (fifteen) and Rutherford (sixteen). Written by Phillips for his first girlfriend when he was thirteen, this was reworked with lyrics following the original melody used here and became 'In Hiding'. Gabriel is credited as playing the drums on this piece. It was released on the *Genesis Archive 1967-1975* set.

'Hey!' 2:28 (Genesis)

This is a demo recorded on 13 March 1968 but not developed for the album. It is quite a strong song with a catchy, frequent use of 'Hey!' that is very reminiscent of the music being released at the time by The Rolling Stones, The Kinks and The Who.

'She is Beautiful' 3:47 (Genesis)

This is an early acoustic demo recorded in 1967, the original version of which from the tape passed to King was supposedly the track that caught his attention due to Gabriel's voice. New lyrics were added, and this became 'The Serpent', one of two tracks from the original tape to make it to an album release. This original demo was released on the *Genesis Archive 1967-1975* set.

Trespass (1970)

Personnel:
Peter Gabriel: lead vocals, flute, accordion, tambourine, bass drum
Anthony Phillips: acoustic 12-string guitar, lead electric guitar, dulcimer, vocals
Anthony Banks: organ, piano, Mellotron, acoustic 12-string guitar, vocals
Michael Rutherford: acoustic 12-string guitar, electric bass guitar, nylon
guitar, cello, vocals
John Mayhew: drums, percussion, vocals
Recorded at Trident Studios, London between June and July 1970
Producer: John Anthony
Sleeve design: Paul Whitehead
Released: 23 October 1970
Label: Charisma
Highest Chart places: UK: 98 (for one week only in 1984), US: Did not chart.
Number 1 in Belgium.
Running time: 42:24

Having turned professional in August 1969, the band spent the winter in the
wonderfully-named Christmas Cottage in Dorking. Richard MacPhail's parents
owned the cottage, and he was now the band's roadie, even though they
hadn't played a gig at this stage and he didn't have a driving licence. John
Mayhew had been recruited as the band's third drummer in as many years
after the departure of Silver. So, in January 1970, having written and rehearsed
in the cottage, they played their first gig at Brunel University, followed by
performances at a string of local clubs including the Marquee where the band
were supporting Rare Bird, who were signed to Charisma and had become the
first band to release an album on the label. Graham Field, Rare Bird's keyboard
player, and producer John Anthony liked Genesis enough to recommend that
the owner of Charisma, Tony Stratton-Smith (Strat) check them out, which he
did with John and also Gail Colson of Charisma while Genesis were playing
a residency upstairs at Ronnie Scott's in Soho. Colson remembers that there
were five people in the band and six in the audience; however, they must have
been impressed since, despite the small attendance, the band were signed to
the label forthwith.

They entered Trident studios, in June 1970 to record *Trespass* which was
completed over the next month. By this point, the songs had been honed over
many live performances, and there was enough material for two LPs, with at
least eight songs not making it onto the record. Several of these discarded
songs were later released as part of the *Genesis Archive 1967-1975* box set.

While all the music is once again simply credited to Genesis, they continued
to write in the original pairs of Banks and Gabriel, and Rutherford and Phillips
and the rest of the band would then develop these ideas further. As the songs
had been played live many times, the recorded material was largely the same as
the live versions with relatively few additions or changes to take advantage of

the recording studio environment.

Before the release, however, Phillips announced he was going to leave the band. He was finding the pressure of live performances too much and suffered from severe stage fright. He later said that he would panic about not being able to remember the music. He would be on stage looking at his guitar and thinking, 'how am I doing this?'. He had also recently suffered from glandular fever without realising that it stays in your system for a while which could easily have contributed to his stage fright and at around this time he also contracted Bronchial Pneumonia and was advised by his doctor to take time out to recover. It is important to remember the ages of the band at the time. By this time, Banks and Gabriel were the oldest at twenty, Rutherford was nineteen and Phillips was still only eighteen, so the decision to continue was not an easy one, with Banks believing that Phillips was vital in the formation of the group and was in many ways their strongest member. Rutherford recalls that this was the closest they ever came to 'busting up', saying: 'Of all the changes the band went through, surviving Ant leaving was the hardest.'

Phillips' influence is evident across the whole of Trespass on both acoustic and lead guitars, and that influence would linger long after he left. A decision was eventually made to carry on, but only on the understanding that a new guitarist and a new drummer were found. Mayhew 'didn't fit in' according to Banks and was the least experienced, with his drum parts worked out for him by others in the band, so he was dismissed, and the remaining three members started the search for a new guitarist and drummer.

In August 1970 Phil Collins spotted an ad for 'a drummer sensitive to acoustic music' and a 'twelve string acoustic guitarist'. He recognised Tony Stratton-Smith's name on the advert and knowing he owned Charisma, applied alongside fellow Flaming Youth member guitarist Ronnie Caryl. They drove to Gabriel's parents' house in Chobham, Surrey in Caryl's Morris Minor, filled with a Gretsch drum kit, guitar and amp. Having arrived early and gone for a swim in the outdoor pool, Collins heard some of the earlier auditions and so was well prepared for his own performance. He was offered the job, Banks claiming that he got the position because he had the best jokes, while Gabriel claims that he knew as soon as Collins sat at his kit, that this was 'the guy'. Collins was on board two months before the release of Trespass which sold 6,000 copies at the time, helping to boost attendances at the band's gigs. Caryl was unsuccessful, however, and Rutherford said later that he didn't think he was a good fit and was more of a blues player. Caryl would later reunite with Collins to tour with him from 1996 onwards.

Trespass was the first of three album covers to be designed by Paul Whitehead, an English artist and graphic designer. The band's producer John Anthony saw some of Whitehead's work in an art show in the West End of London and contacted him with regards working on a design. Whitehead stayed with the band during some of the writing sessions and developed a good relationship with them which continued for the next two releases.

The cover itself was based on themes from the five originally planned songs, 'The Knife' being added to the album at a late stage. The band wanted the cover reworked, but Whitehead was reluctant to do so, so they convinced him to slash the canvas with a real dagger and use a photo of the result. The room lighting caused the blue hue of the cover when the photo was taken. Whitehead claims the reason that there were only three covers with Genesis and not more was his move to America – working across transatlantic boundaries in the 1970s wasn't as easy as it is today. Whitehead would go on to design covers for other Charisma artists, such as Van der Graaf Generator and their singer Peter Hammill's solo releases and he also played the drums on Hammill's *Fool's Mate* album. Charisma retained the original art for the three covers, but, sadly, the paintings were stolen at the time when the label was sold to Virgin Records in 1983. According to Whitehead, when the Charisma staff got wind of the sale, 'they just looted the place'. He later recreated all three paintings for a show in Milan, working from the LP covers.

'Looking for Someone' 7:04 (Genesis)

From the opening bars of the first track, it is clear this is a different Genesis from the debut release. The desire to create a more complex, unique sound coupled with the development of the music at live gigs brings a whole new level of maturity to the music. After the opening vocal 'Looking for someone', sung over a quiet organ, the bass, drums and guitar are introduced gradually over the first minute. This effect holds the listener's attention as the track unfolds, and over the full seven minutes, we are treated to a piece that changes multiple times, full of dynamic key and tempo changes. Phillips impresses particularly, playing multiple lead guitar parts and the song begins to gallop at around three minutes, before opening up into a new theme, then slowing once again via Gabriel's flute and Banks' piano. Another theme is introduced at 4:30 before organ, flute and guitar solos are used to build toward the finale, via another slow passage. The ending showcases guitar, flute and piano through to a satisfying and dramatic climax, most likely written with live performance in mind, and avoiding a fade out. Given the number of changes and themes in a relatively short song 'Looking for someone' has a genuinely epic feel to it. The idea of piecing together lots of shorter 'bits' to make a longer piece is one that would be used regularly by the band, and other early exponents of progressive rock.

'White Mountain' 6:40 (Genesis)

Based loosely on the book *White Fang* by Jack London, the story follows on from 'One-Eyed Hound', the B-side from 'A Winter's Tale'. Fang is a wild wolf-dog hybrid and is the son of One-Eye. It is the first of many songs by the band to illustrate its story by the creation of atmosphere to help take the listener on an emotional journey. After the power of the opening piece, this initially slows things down with an airy multiple twelve-string guitar section which would become one of the band's signature sounds. This quiet interlude continues into the first verse before drums enter for the second. Rather than give us a chorus, the song returns to the acoustic section several times, alternating with the faster, almost galloping, tempo. Returning to the guitar and organ theme briefly for a melodic solo from Gabriel on flute, the pattern of light and shade carries us to the second half of the song, where a slow drum beat signals another change in tonality until Gabriel sings 'he the usurper must die' taking us into the 'fight' section. The only disappointment is the section at 5:25 which features Gabriel whistling along to an organ backing for 30 seconds which adds nothing to the structure of the song, and if anything detracts from the quality of the other sections. After this unnecessary diversion, we return to the rich guitar anthem once again to a finish.

'Visions of Angels' 6:48 (Genesis)
Originally written for *From Genesis To Revelation* by Philips but not recorded at the time, this is reminiscent of those earlier songs but is permitted to develop without the restrictions of King's production. The composition follows a simpler format, in only two parts – the vocal and the strong instrumental sections used in the middle and end of the piece. Everything is thrown at this big theme in both sections, featuring Banks on Mellotron, piano and organ, creating a hugely dramatic ending. The only thing missing is lead guitar which might have rounded the piece off in fine style. Mayhew plays well on this, as he generally does on *Trespass*.

'Stagnation' 8:46 (Genesis)
Gabriel describes this as a 'journey' song as opposed to having a standard song structure, and it drifts through various 'landscapes' of sound. It tells the story of a nuclear war where there is only one survivor. The original sleeve lyrics includes an additional introduction:

To Thomas S. Eiselberg, a very rich man, who was wise enough to spend all his fortunes in burying himself many miles beneath the ground. As the only surviving member of the human race, he inherited the whole world.

The longest – and stand out – track on *Trespass*, it begins with several guitar-backed themes in pastoral style and understated vocals from Gabriel before a plaintive organ solo from Banks that shows how much he was already experimenting with the instrument to push it to its limits. At times it sounds more like a synthesiser than an organ with bent notes created by turning off the organ which caused the tone wheels to slow down, while the valve amp would still work for a few seconds as the valves cooled. At just over three minutes in we have the first example of a full-on Genesis theme pushing the piece forward before returning to the quiet Gabriel vocal and a multi-tracked vocal choir. This is paired with more multi-tracked guitar, including ten twelve-string guitars at one point, although Rutherford says they ended up cancelling each other out so that you couldn't hear anything properly. The end section at 6:55 builds again, with the main melody played on flute until drums re-enter at 7:35 for the climax. The end section was often used on early live versions of 'I Know What I Like'.

'Dusk' 4:11 (Genesis)

The shortest and most acoustic track is based around a warm arrangement of multiple layered twelve and six string acoustic guitars which have an almost harp-like quality, it is perfectly placed between the two finest pieces on the album and is a perfect set up for 'The Knife'. Originally titled 'Family', Phillips later revealed that the lyrics were about someone who was facing his end through cancer. The words aren't too literal, but there are some lovely phrases such as 'A false move by God will now destroy me', 'And now my ship is sinking, the captain stands alone' and the final lines 'But wait, on the horizon, a new dawn seems to be rising. Never to recall this passerby, born to die.' An early demo version of the song, close to its finished form recorded in August 1969, is included on the *Genesis Archive 1967-75* compilation. The only piece not to feature any drums, Mayhew plays finger bells, while the song relies on the rich texture created by the mix of guitars, organ, harmonies and Gabriel's breathy flute solo. 'Dusk' is often overlooked on *Trespass* but really deserves another listen if you haven't played it for a while.

'The Knife' 8:55 (Genesis)

This track was based on an idea from Banks and Gabriel called 'The Nice' as a reference to Keith Emerson's group at the time, who were also signed to Charisma. At the time of recording *Trespass,* Emerson was already rocking his organ and using a knife to hold down keys on his Hammond to create a sustained drone note. The second world war German dagger he often used was given to him by Lemmy Kilmister, who was a roadie for The Nice and Jimi Hendrix before joining Hawkwind and later forming Motorhead.

After the relative serenity of most of the music so far, 'The Knife' shows a more aggressive, rocking side to Genesis that translated well to the live gigs and showed their ability to move away from the folky, twelve-string 'goblins, fairies and unicorns' of some of their other work. There is no slow build up on this one, as it starts with Banks' vamping organ theme and is quickly running at full speed into Gabriel's tongue-twisting lyrics. The guitars from Phillips throughout are a highlight and at 2:54 we are treated to harmony guitars playing the main theme backed by Banks on organ which itself breaks for a brief flute solo before we get Gabriel on modified vocals singing the 'We are only wanting freedom' section at 4:37. The call of 'OK men, fire over their heads' and a girl's scream announce the start of the best solo Phillips recorded with Genesis, pausing again at 7:00 for an organ break to change the pace for the ending with Phillips on heavy distorted guitar. The announcement and screams were references to the tragic Ohio shootings in 1970 where National Guardsmen were told to shoot over the heads of students protesting against Nixon's bombing of Cambodia. Four students were killed, and nine were wounded. One of the more exciting tracks for the band to play live, it could often reach nineteen minutes in length.

The track was released as the only single from *Trespass*, split across both A and B-sides, in May 1971 but failed to enter the charts. Always a fan favourite, calls for 'The Knife' were still being heard from audiences many years after Gabriel's departure.

Related tracks:
Several other songs were considered for *Trespass*, with the band having enough material for a double LP at the time. Many like 'Everywhere is Here', 'Grandma', 'Little Leaf' and 'Moss' appear to have been lost forever, but several others exist, some of which were recorded for radio broadcast and released on the *Genesis Archive 1967 – 1975* collection. They are included here to illustrate the transitional nature of the bands writing around this time.

'Shepherd' 4:04 (Genesis)
This is a simple song which starts with Banks playing rising piano chords that are similar to those that would be used later on 'Heathaze'. Also notable for Banks singing the chorus, the song was recorded for the BBC *Nightride* radio program and broadcast on 22 February 1970. It was probably the correct decision to leave this off *Trespass* as it is clearly a transitional song, belonging to the *From Genesis To Revelation* era.

'Pacidy' 5:44 (Genesis)
'Pacidy' is a song like 'Shepherd', containing mostly a simple guitar backing with sprinkles of flute and organ. Another piece recorded for the BBC *Nightride* program that never made it to album, only the end section stands up as the rest of the song is weak compared with the other material on *Trespass*.

'Let Us Now Make Love' 6:16 (Genesis)
Another of the *Nightride* recordings, this song is even more pastoral than the other non-released tracks. The flute introduction and solos are fine, but the song is drawn out for over six minutes without any good reason.

'Going Out to Get You' 4:54 (Genesis)
This is a demo recorded on 20 August 1969 at Regent Sound Studio, five months after the release of *From Genesis To Revelation*. This was the last demo session recorded while the band were still under the management of King and contracted to Decca records. It is a follow on from some of the folky pop songs on the debut recording, but with a slightly edgier feel to it.

'Provocation' 4:10 (Genesis)
This is an early version of 'Looking For Someone'. The organ and guitar sections are similar, but the arrangement and the melody are quite different with several sections that aren't present in the final track. It was recorded for a BBC documentary in 1970 about painter Michael Jackson which was never broadcast.

Nursery Cryme (1971)

Personnel:
Tony Banks' organ, Mellotron, piano, electric piano, 12-string guitar, voices
Mike Rutherford: bass, bass pedals, 12-string guitar, voices
Peter Gabriel: lead voice, flute, oboe, bass drum, tambourine
Steve Hackett: electric guitar, 12-string guitar
Phil Collins: drums, voices, percussion, lead voice on 'For Absent Friends' (uncredited)
Recorded at Trident Studios, London in August 1971
Producer: John Anthony
Sleeve design: Paul Whitehead
Released: 12 November 1971
Label: Charisma
Highest Chart places: UK: 39, US: Did not chart. Reached number four in the Italian charts. Achieved gold in France (50,000 copies) and silver in the UK (60,000 copies).
Running time: 39:26

After the release of *Trespass*, the band continued to play live as a four piece for several months. Banks would play two keyboards at the same time, using a Hohner Pianet through a fuzz box to make up for the lack of guitar, which also helped hone his playing technique. In order to allow him to play rhythm guitar live without losing bass, Rutherford started using bass pedals which would become another signature sound – and sight – of the band. He now wonders if they would ever have used them, had playing as four-piece not necessitated it during that period. During this time, the basis for 'The Musical Box' was developed. There was certainly volatility in rehearsals around this time, with Rutherford or Banks often storming out, leaving Collins to wonder what he had joined, often cracking a joke to break the tension.

Mick Barnard was briefly added on guitar, but the band felt he wasn't good enough and continued to look for a replacement. Collins' abiding memory of Barnard was not his playing, but that Mick was always dropped off at Toddington services on the M1 near Dunstable after gigs. Collins has no idea to this day how he got home from there. At this point, the band played between 120 and 130 shows over that year, mostly as a support act or headlining in smaller venues, often with small audiences. Banks remembers that they played to three people at one venue, although Phillips remembers an audience of one during his time in the band.

In December 1970, Gabriel spotted an ad in the Melody Maker:

Imaginative Guitarist/writer seeks involvement with receptive musicians determined to strive beyond existing stagnant music forms. – Steve 730 2445

Steve Hackett, who had been placing similar ads for almost five years, was invited to Banks' new flat in Earls Court. He arrived dressed all in black, impressed everyone and was offered the job in January 1971, playing his first gig on 24 January at University College, London.

Hackett came onboard close to the recording of *Nursery Cryme*, with 'The Musical Box' for example, having been in development while Phillips was still with the band. Most of the guitar parts had been developed further by Barnard, so Hackett started where Barnard left off and tried to make his own contributions to the established parts. The timing of the recording sessions also meant that Hackett's opportunity for writing material was limited – he could only provide 'bits' and try to add guitar support to the vocals and keyboards. He did, however, suggest that Banks purchase a Mellotron which was to become such a major part of the band's sound. They visited Robert Fripp of King Crimson and bought a spare one from him. It was called the 'Black Bitch' on account of its tendency to break down regularly, and Hackett remembers that it required four people to lift it. The MKI and MKII units had a built-in amplifier as well as two twelve-inch speakers and weighed a staggering 160kg or 351 pounds. Later, the classic M400 units were 'only' 55 kg or 122 lbs.

Due to a busy touring schedule, it was difficult to find the time to work on new ideas, so in order to allocate a period to write the album, the group spent time at Luxford House in Crowborough, East Sussex which was owned by Tony Stratton-Smith. Almost three months were taken out during the summer of 1971 to complete *Nursery Cryme*, with the band going back to Trident Studios in London to record the material in August.

Even though the quality of the music, musicianship and the recording on the album were significantly better than *Trespass*, sales of *Nursery Cryme* were pretty much the same as its predecessor. It did peak at number 39 in the UK charts, but not until three years after release. It also reached number four in the Italian charts and would eventually reach silver album status for 60,000 sales in the UK some 42 years later. It isn't a great album, though it does contain two great songs in 'The Musical Box' and 'The Fountain of Salmacis'. In retrospect, it is best to regard this as a transition album, containing parts which were started by Phillips, with Collins and Hackett finding their feet with the material while also making important contributions. Collins' drumming is bold and inventive, as displayed on 'The Musical Box' and 'Return Of The Giant Hogweed', but also shows a restrained, delicate touch on the quieter sections of 'Seven Stones' and 'The Fountain Of Salmacis'. Hackett not only delivers powerful signature solos on 'The Musical Box' and 'The Fountain Of Salmacis' but also demonstrates his acoustic prowess on 'For Absent Friends'.

Charisma didn't really promote the album, giving it even less attention than they had *Trespass*, as they were putting their weight behind Lindisfarne's *Fog On The Tyne* at the time. Genesis had already toured with Lindisfarne, also supporting Van Der Graaf Generator earlier in 1971 and would support the band from the northeast again as *Fog On The Tyne* worked its way towards number one in the UK charts in 1972.

During the tour of the album, the band recorded 'Happy the Man' which was released as a single with 'Seven Stones' as the B-side on 12 May 1972 with little success. The album is also notable for the participation of David Hentschel as engineer. He would later produce a string of four albums starting with *A Trick of the Tail* and continuing until *Duke*. It was also the second cover designed by Paul Whitehead, and he also created a new Genesis logo that would be used on this and another two albums, *Foxtrot* and *Genesis Live*.

'The Musical Box' 10:28 (Genesis)

For the rest of their career, this was to be one of their best-loved tracks, particularly the ending that would later be used as part of a medley of older songs. It allowed Gabriel to play the character of Henry on stage and was one of the first songs that would inspire him to wear masks and costumes, despite often having a detrimental effect on his live vocals. Gabriel often explained the story behind the song during performances:

> *Henry Hamilton-Smythe, aged eight, had been playing croquet with Cynthia Jane De Blaise-William, aged nine, when she took off Henry's head with her croquet mallet. Henry's spirit went skyward, but returned, rejected, left awaiting the opening of his old musical box. Two weeks later Cynthia finds Henry's musical box, and, curious, opens it. As it plays 'Old King Cole', Henry's spirit enters the room but immediately starts to grow old, experiencing a lifetime of sexual desires. Henry's advances raise the attention of the nanny who throws the musical box at Henry's spirit, destroying both.*

'The Musical Box' remains one of the most accomplished of Genesis' compositions, telling a complete story but musically moving through several sections of light and shade. The opening twelve-string guitar part was an older idea from Rutherford and Phillips in which the top three strings were tuned to F#. Indeed, the song started its life called 'F Sharp'. Hackett had recently joined when this was recorded and realising that nobody was playing anything like a musical box on the song, he added a short, high-pitched guitar riff which was speeded up and can be heard just after the words 'play me my song'.

Choosing to start the first side of the album quietly, in the same way as *Trespass*, the opening twelve-string guitar section is joined by Gabriel's vocal and some light lead guitar. This section gently serenades the listener until the much brasher, louder section kicks in at 3:38 as guitar, drums and organ join in. The heavier guitar parts were added at the request of Gabriel who was a big fan of The Who and wanted Pete Townsend-style, arm swinging energy on the song. Hackett boldly announces his presence with a storming solo before we return to the quiet verse and a reprise of 'Old King Cole'. The second instrumental section is very much in the style of 'The Knife', with fuzzed organ and guitar solos, while the quiet guitar 'she's a lady' section is one of the most memorable parts of the piece, often played as part of the 'old medley' in later gigs. The piece ends with on a big finish after 'I've been waiting here for so long' gives way to the 'Now, Now, Now, Now!' calls and Hackett's harmony guitar coda. Once again, the opening track doesn't waste any time letting us know we have an updated, more confident and tighter sound, particularly with the huge improvement in drums and guitars.

'For Absent Friends' 1:46 (Genesis)

This simple, short guitar and vocal song is memorable for two reasons: firstly, this is Collins' debut on lead vocal, and secondly, it was the first piece written by Hackett for Genesis. Hackett and Collins wrote the lyrics and Collins sang it to the band so they could hear the melody. His debut went mostly unnoticed as the performance wasn't credited on the album sleeve and Collins' voice does sound rather similar to Gabriel on the song. It tells of two friends, both widowed, and how they were 'looking back at days of four instead of two', 'Heads bent in prayer. For friends not there'. There's a suggestion that the new boys in the band were being offered scraps from the table even in 1971. Stylistically, the song harks back to some of their earlier material, with multiple layered guitars and piano and Collins does well for his first lead, demonstrating his vocal range with a pleasing softness to his voice. However, nothing about the song really stands out, and it is often forgotten or skipped by listeners. However, given what was to happen to Collins as the vocalist in years to come, it's an important piece.

'The Return of the Giant Hogweed' 8:12 (Genesis)

This track tells the story of how a Victorian explorer finds the Hogweed, Heracleum Mantegazzianum in the Russian Hills and brings it back to the Royal Gardens at Kew. From there, however, it spreads, immune to herbicides and threatening the human race with extinction. The highlight here is the first example of Hackett 'tapping', playing the guitar neck with both hands and tapping the fingers on the fretboard, in a similar way to a keyboard. Another upbeat, organ-driven song, similar to 'The Knife,' it suffers more than a little from 'lyric bloat' with a melody and lyrics added after the music was written, leading to something of a jumble of words. Just before the five-minute point, Banks plays an arpeggio chord sequence combined with Pink Floyd style reverberated guitar that changes the mood and pace of the song for the better until the vocals return us to Victorian England for the end of the story. It is a somewhat average piece for this era of the band, but it feels like a necessary step as the band learned how to develop its storytelling skills and hone its complex, multi-part arrangements.

'Seven Stones' 5:10 (Genesis)

An organ intro, not unlike Procul Harum, introduces this slow ballad which feels deceptively simple given that it has at least four different keys, somewhat typical of the band at the time, who were looking to avoid the expected and show their prowess as musicians. Banks wrote the music and lyrics, and stylistically, the song owes much to the earlier material on *Trespass* and to a lesser extent, those on *From Genesis To Revelation*. A challenging melody line sets this song apart for the rest of the album as it weaves through several different sections including a lovely flute solo from Gabriel. The first rendition of the chorus is delivered as a bold proclamation 'Despair that tires the world brings the old man laughter', but the second time around with a quieter, more subdued delivery. One of the highlights of the number is the fantastic Mellotron chord progression that ends the song, recorded a full one year before the iconic introduction to 'Watcher Of The Skies.' The song was released as the B-side to the single 'Happy The Man' in May 1972, but failed to chart.

'Harold the Barrel' 2:59 (Genesis)

Written by Gabriel at the piano, 'Harold The Barrel' tells the tale of the titular Harold, who climbs up to the top of a building, threatening to throw himself off. It continues with the resulting media attention and the reaction of his mother and the public to these events. Much of the song is sung by Gabriel and Collins together as a duet, and it is quite astonishing how many words Gabriel crams into a song that is just under three minutes long. This is one of several 'comic' songs that appear on the early releases contrasting with the often serious and even high brow nature of the lyrics in other songs. The track ends with some slow piano chords as if to change tempo and move to another section, but in fact, fades out just as Harold 'jumps'.

'Harlequin' 2:56 (Genesis)

Harlequin is the last of the three short songs. Rutherford wrote it in the style that he pioneered with Phillips, given the double twelve-string guitars. The most memorable part of the song is the first line 'Came the night a mist dissolved the trees' which conjures up images of a late autumn sunset. Collins' vocals are again prominent on this song.

'The Fountain of Salmacis' 7:55 (Genesis)

This piece and 'Musical Box' make up the best music on the album. The piece tells the legend of the Greek Hermaphroditus, born of Hermes and Aphrodite. Mythology tells of how Hermaphroditus, having both sexes, was born remarkably handsome and the nymph Salmacis fell in love with him, praying to be united with him forever.

The short introduction makes good use of waves of Mellotron, organ and guitar before the verse starts. The instrumental break halfway through provides a heavier section with Banks on distorted organ supported by Hackett's lead guitar, which is followed by a more melodic section featuring organ and flute. Hackett, who had already established a style of playing and a sound that would continue throughout his time with Genesis, provides a great solo at the end of this song, which quickly became a live favourite.

Related tracks:

'Happy The Man' 3.08 (Genesis)

Released as a single in 1972 with 'Seven Stones' as the B-side, this song was an attempt at a hit single. Propelled by a simple twelve-string acoustic guitar riff, and not much else, this pleasant but generic pop song links directly back to the material on *From Genesis To Revelation*. The melody, sung by Gabriel, is strong but it's no surprise that the song failed to trouble the charts.

'Manipulation' 3:49 (Genesis)

This song was recorded for a BBC documentary in 1970 about painter Michael Jackson which was never broadcast. The song contains sections of what would later become 'Musical Box' on *Nursery Cryme*. It was released on the *Genesis 1970-1975* box set.

Foxtrot (1972)

Personnel:
Tony Banks: Hammond Organ, Mellotron, electric and acoustic pianos, 12-string guitar, backing vocals
Steve Hackett: electric guitar, nylon guitar, 12-string guitar
Phil Collins: drums, backing vocals, assorted percussion
Peter Gabriel: lead vocals, flute, bass drum, tambourine, oboe
Mike Rutherford: bass guitar, bass pedals, cello, 12-string guitar, backing vocals
Recorded at Island Studios, London between August and September 1972
Producer: David Hitchcock
Sleeve design: Paul Whitehead
Released: 6 October 1972
Label: Charisma
Highest Chart places: UK: 12, US: Did not chart. Reached number 1 in the Italian charts. Achieved gold in the UK (100,000) and France (50,000).
Running time: 51:08

A stable line up is never guaranteed with Genesis and while this would be the band's fourth release, it was the first time they would enter the recording studio with the same line-up as the previous album. After extensive touring in support of *Nursery Cryme* both Hackett and Collins were threatening to leave the band. Having spent time rehearsing in the basement of Una Billings School for dance in Shepherd Bush, they recorded the album in Island Studios, a converted church in Notting Hill, where both *Led Zeppelin IV* and Jethro Tull's *Aqualung* had been recorded two years earlier. Charisma records owner Tony Stratton-Smith recalls his reaction on first hearing the completed version:

This is the one that makes their career. I had to wipe a tear from my eye. Everything that one had believed about the band had come through.

Banks has since commented that the production was 'something of a farce' due to several personnel changes during the recording process. Bob Potter, a talented engineer but new to production, started the album but didn't really 'get' the band, commenting that he didn't like the opening chords of 'Watcher of The Skies' and didn't think they should use the track. David Hitchcock was then brought in as the producer, and John Burns came in to engineer. The band worked well with Burns, particularly in the later stages of completing 'Supper's Ready' and he would go on to produce *Selling England by the Pound,* and *The Lamb Lies Down On Broadway* with him. Hitchcock 'was there but he wasn't very important' and wasn't used by the band again. On top of the production changes, the band took several breaks from recording to go on the road, including shows at the Reading festival, the Bilsen festival in Belgium and a two-week tour of Italy.

It was at this time, about a week before the release of Foxtrot, that while playing 'The Musical Box' at the National Stadium in Dublin, Gabriel returned to the stage after the second solo section wearing his wife's red dress and a fox's head, in the style of the cover of Foxtrot. This was the first costume to be worn live on stage and was as much a surprise to the band as it was to the audience. Gabriel hadn't told them, as he expected that Banks would veto it if he did. Further costumes would be added, such as the flower mask for 'Willow Farm', the triangular head for 'Apocalypse in 9/8' and the batwing for 'Watcher of the Skies', all of which the band saw for the first time at the same time as the audience. It had the desired effect, with the press widely reporting it and Gabriel appearing on the front cover of the *Melody Maker*, which immediately increased ticket sales. Collins comments that it added a zero to their booking fee – they went from getting £35 a gig to a £350 a gig after that front-page story was published.

The cover was the last of the Paul Whitehead designs, and the one with which the band were least happy. In interviews, all commented on how busy it was, with its 2D collage texture and how it didn't reflect the content of the album itself. Indeed, Whitehead quotes Jimi Hendrix's 'Foxy Lady' as the inspiration for the cover.

'Watcher of the Skies' 7:21 (Genesis)

While Banks had used the Mellotron MKII on the previous two albums, he had been working out which chords sound best on the instrument, and these formed the introduction to this famous track.

The title for the song is taken from the John Keats poem 'On First Looking into Chapman's Homer', specifically the lines 'Then I felt like some watcher of the skies when a new planet swims into his ken'. The song tells the story of a superior being who has been overseeing earth – watching the planet from afar. The lyrics were also inspired by the novel *Childhood's End* by Arthur C. Clarke, the author of the short story 'The Sentinel' from which he then wrote the book and co-wrote the script with director Stanley Kubrick, for the 1968 movie *2001: A Space Odyssey*.

The Mellotron intro is the star of the piece here, ratcheting up the tension towards the first verse and was an effective, atmospheric opener for many live gigs. The Morse code-type beats, reminiscent of 'Mars' from Holst's *The Planets*, drive the track forward. The vocal sections suffer from either too many words or not enough notes (whichever way you want to look at it) – something of a stumbling tongue twister, especially in the verses. Hackett plays a memorable solo with the band partway through the song – bettered only by 'Firth Of Fifth' from *Selling England By The Pound* which is, perhaps, his best.

A shortened version was released as a single with 'Willow Farm' as the B-side on 6 October 1972 but failed to chart. The cover of that single had pictures of the five band members, plus Richard MacPhail, by then their tour manager.

'Time Table' 4:47 (Genesis)

This is a simple song that takes us back, tonally, to *From Genesis To Revelation* and halcyon days of knights, maidens and chivalry. It clearly has nothing to do with a timetable or school schedule as many believe. It seems to be a play on words, comparing the different pace of life between 1972 and medieval times. The lyrics tell us that 'A carved oak table tells a tale' and 'A dusty table, musty smells', evoking an image of someone entering an old stately home or castle. Upon looking at an old, worn table, their imagination takes them on a journey in time to conjure up thoughts of who would have sat there and how different life was in those days. 'Of times when kings and queens sipped wine from goblets gold' and 'A time when honour meant much more to a man than life'.

The piano introduction does sound a bit like an academic grading exercise. It is slightly medieval in feel, consistent with the period covered in the lyrics, but it might have been omitted without damaging the piece. The song's chorus lifts the track via a catchy repetition of 'Why', while the short, piano and bass instrumental section in the middle and towards the end of the piece, most likely written by Banks, hints at a style of his writing that would appear again on albums later in the 1970s.

'Get 'em Out by Friday' 8:35 (Genesis)

This is a song about bad landlords and is inspired by Peter Rachman and his exploitation of tenants in London during the 1950s and 1960s. It also explores the rather surreal idea that if you could genetically shrink the population to be under four feet, you could fit more people in the same space – a theme later developed in a 2017 movie starring Matt Damon.

Gabriel uses voices to act out several characters in the story including John Pebble and Mark Hall of Styx Enterprises, and tenant Mrs Barrow. Once again, he battles to get as many words as possible into the song – rather more than it really requires.

The quiet middle section has a lovely duet between Mellotron and real flute which marks a 'passage of time' as noted in the sleeve notes to bring us to 2012, then 40 years in the future, a caustic reminder of how long ago the album was recorded. The song also features one of Rutherford's most intricate baselines an interesting contrast with some of the simple single note bass parts used on later albums, especially Abacab.

'Can-Utility and the Coastliners' 5:45 (Genesis)

This track features another of the many puns in Genesis lyrics and song titles, 'Can-Ut'ility being King Canute the Danish King of the North Sea empire in the early 11th century, with 'coastliners' referring to his delusion that he was master of all and could even command the sea to turn back.

Written mostly by Hackett, it had been played already as a longer piece live entitled 'Bye Johnny' or 'Rock My Baby'. The guitar and Mellotron introduction provides a mellow backing for Gabriel before the drums enter and drive the song towards some excellent mini-peaks, followed by a new acoustic guitar instrumental part augmented by Mellotron. The last two minutes of the song are the most satisfying as the organ and Mellotron chords dominate, in a style that would again return in later releases. Solos by Banks and Hackett take us to the final vocal section as this song ends side one of the vinyl album.

'Horizons' 1:39 (Genesis)

Although every track on the album is credited to the band, this is obviously a Hackett composition – a solo classical guitar piece showing just how good a classical guitarist he was even in 1972. Sometimes mistaken as the first part of 'Supper's Ready', it is a standalone piece that opens the second side of the original vinyl album. It was based on the *Prelude from Suite No. 1 in G Major for cello* by Johann Sebastian Bach. The original piece has been used in numerous TV and film scores such as *The Pianist, Ex Machina* and *Master and Commander.*

It is 99 seconds of pure magic, played in standard tuning on only one classical nylon string guitar with great use of harmonics. It is still played live by Hackett who was genuinely surprised that it made it onto the album, although when he first played it to the band, Collins said he felt there should be applause at the end of it.

'Supper's Ready' 22:57 (Genesis)

This classic piece can be considered something of an accidental, or opportunistic epic. When the track was being written, a 23-minute piece wasn't something the band were planning. The first four sections were pieced together from ideas that were being worked on separately by the band. However, jumping into 'Willow Farm', a complete song already written by Gabriel, lifts the track to a larger-scale, storytelling piece of music, but one which was now in need of an ending. The length of the piece was a cause for concern at the time, as the longer the track length, the tighter together the grooves on the vinyl album had to be, which meant the output volume would to be lower. Gabriel still sees this and *The Lamb Lies Down On Broadway* as his best work from his time with the band.

Aside from the 'Willow Farm' section, Gabriel wrote the lyrics and most of the vocal melodies after the music had been written. He quotes *The Pilgrim's Progress* by John Bunyan as inspiration for the overarching story, something he would return to with *The Lamb Lies Down On Broadway*. Gabriel also cites that an influence for the lyrics at the start of the piece came from an other-worldly experience shared with his girlfriend Jill and John Anthony when they were at her parent's flat in Kensington Palace. Apparently, her face changed, and she started talking in a strange voice. When Gabriel created a makeshift cross with a candlestick and another item in the room, as he had seen in Hammer horror movies, she became violent. Looking out of the window, the lawn had somehow changed, and he saw seven ghost-like figures walking across it. There are many religious references in the lyrics, harking back to Gabriel's Church of England schooling at Charterhouse.

The first time I saw this performed live was in July 1976 during the A Trick of the Tail tour. In those days there was no internet and so no setlist spoilers and the music press was one of the only ways to find out about gigs, albums or to read reviews. You can imagine the cheer that went up when Rutherford said 'Which brings us to the next song. It's a short little ditty entitled "Supper's Ready"', only to be bettered by the roar of applause 24 minutes later after the rollercoaster of emotions that the piece produces.

'i. Lover's Leap' (00:00 – 3:47)

The epic begins with Hackett, Rutherford and Banks on 12 string guitars, joined later by Banks on electric piano and finally with a multi-tracked choir. This is a slow, smouldering start, with no lead guitar or drums, but it sets the scene and leaves the listener wanting to hear more. The line 'I swear I saw your face change, it didn't seem quite right' refers to the supernatural experience Gabriel had with Jill and John Anthony. The hero of our story has been away from his lover for some time and has returned to her embrace. For there on, their reunion goes downhill as they are sucked into another world, in a lyrical theme that would recur in *The Lamb Lies Down On Broadway*.

'ii. The Guaranteed Eternal Sanctuary Man' (3:48 – 5:43)

We don't need to wait too long for the first of many musical peaks, and it comes with the full Genesis wall of sound. Only a few minutes into the epic and we already we have a dilemma between good and evil, in the form of a farmer, who is nurturing the crops 'with water clear' and a fireman (The Guaranteed Eternal Sanctuary Man) who 'looks after the fire'. The end of the section has a short verse sung by children 'We will rock you, rock you little boat, we will keep you snug and warm'. There were eight children brought in from 'the street' to sing this part, each paid the princely sum of ten bob – ten shillings, or 50p – in modern currency.

'iii. Ikhnaton and Itsacon and Their Band of Merry Men' (5:44 – 9:42)

There is more wordplay in the title here, with 'Itsacon' being, 'It's A Con' and Ikhnaton's armies about to go into battle. Ikhnaton was the tenth pharaoh of the 18th dynasty in Egypt, most famous for fathering Tutankhamun with one of his sisters. He reigned under his original name Amenhotep IV for five years before changing it to reflect his worship of the sun god Aten. He was married to the famous Nefertiti, with whom he had eight daughters and spent most of his reign trying to eradicate the existing gods of the time, especially Ra, and replace them with Aten, another sun god. After his death, everything was returned to the way it was before his reign over a period of ten years, and an attempt was made to erase him from history. The title and the lyrics may then be inspired by the religious battle he fought against the priests of the time, while the people of Egypt believed in his change of gods, so maybe 'it's a con'.

The opening melody from 'Lover Leap' is reprised by Gabriel on flute at the start of this section. This leads to the second musical peak in 'Supper's Ready' with the instrumental battle section leading into an extended Hackett guitar solo including another great example of his tapping technique, playing in time with Banks on organ, before we are slowly brought back down again almost to a halt as the music slows and quietens.

'iv. How Dare I Be So Beautiful' (9:43 – 11:04)

The title of this section harkens back to the early days of the band when Jonathan King would look in the mirror and say, 'How dare I be so beautiful'. Remembering this, Gabriel decided that this would be a great title, referencing Narcissus. Narcissus was cursed by Nemesis the god of revenge to fall in love with his own reflection after Echo committed suicide, having been spurned by Narcissus. Narcissus takes his own life when he cannot have his new-found love and, in his place, grows a yellow and white flower.

The song starts with the aftermath of the previous battle with Gabriel singing plaintively over an almost discordant, swelling guitar. From the vantage point on top of a plateau, we see a lone figure sitting by a pool. In a twist that would be used again on *The Lamb Lies Down On Broadway* we realise that the figure is us 'as we watch in reverence as Narcissus is turned to a flower.'

'v. Willow Farm' (11:05 – 15:36)

Originally a standalone song from Gabriel, 'Willow farm' was added to the middle of 'Supper's Ready' according to Banks, to distinguish it from their earlier epic song 'Stagnation'. It feels completely out of context with the rest of the story, but it provides a lighter moment in an otherwise dark, brooding 23 minutes of music. Like the lighter songs often used in musical theatre, for example 'Master Of The House' in *Les Misérables,* this song is used to give the audience some light relief from a tense storyline.

This is a bouncy interlude which contrasts musically with the rest of the piece just as much as the lyrical content does. The song has two parts, split at the point where the train door slams and the announcement 'all change'. After the main part of 'Willow Farm' is over the song slows to Mellotron, organ and lead guitar before giving way to a beautiful, quiet guitar and flute solo that slowly builds towards a musical reprise of the 'I know a farmer' theme.

'vi. Apocalypse in 9/8 (Co-Starring the Delicious Talents of Gabble Ratchet)' (15:37 – 20:50)

This section starts with ' the guards of Magog, swarming around' section sung over a constant throb of guitar. Beginning after the last line of the lyric 'Better not compromise, it won't be easy,' we enter the 9/8 instrumental section. The first couple of bars are a little off, timing wise, but this is quickly forgiven as the band kicks in and then the main instrumental section marches on with one of Banks' iconic organ solos and Collins playing one of his most complex of drum timings. This is as grand and promenading as Genesis get, almost orchestral in texture. The segue from the organ solo over the 9/8 section to where Banks plays chords and the flute enters at 17:56, works fantastically well as a break in the tension of the relentless throb of the band. With Banks in full flow, Gabriel returns with the '666' lyric. This section caused an issue between Banks and Gabriel during the recording. Banks feeling the section should be a long instrumental and so he was initially annoyed that Gabriel was singing over 'his bit', but he soon realised that it improved the song, later saying: 'That half minute or so is probably our peak.'

We have a host of biblical references here, in particular to the 'Book of Revelations' again with lyrics like '666 is no longer alone', 666 being the mark of the beast or the devil. Magog appears in the Bible and the Quran and is associated with apocalyptic or catastrophic events. 'Seven trumpets blowing sweet rock and roll', refers to the seven trumpets sounded to mark the events of the apocalypse, or the end of the world predicted in the 'Book of Revelations'. However, here I believe Gabriel is referring back to his days at Charterhouse again where rock music was seen as a bad influence on the boys, with Mick Jagger considered the devil incarnate, as if rock and roll were an indication of the pending apocalypse.

Were this section finishes and the last begins is cause for debate. The sleeve notes show this continuing until after the line 'And babe it's gonna work out fine'. Based on that, the section finishes with Mellotron, ready for the grand finale, complete with a hugely emotional Gabriel vocal:

'vii. As Sure As Eggs Is Eggs (Aching Men's Feet)' (20:51 – 22:54)

Revelation 19:17 in the King James version of *the Bible* says:
'And I saw an angel standing in the sun; and he cried with a loud voice, saying to all the fowls that fly in midheaven, Come and gather yourselves together unto the supper of the great God'. Here those words are translated to 'There's an angel standing in the sun. And he's crying with a loud voice. This is the supper of the mighty one'. This is further confirmed in the final lines 'Lord of Lords, King of Kings. Has returned to lead his children home. To take them to the new Jerusalem'. 'King of Kings, Lord of Lords' is used in Revelation 19:16, and is here reversed to 'Lord of Lords, King of Kings' in Revelations 17:14 and refers to Jesus as the ruler over all other Lords and Kings. The 'New Jerusalem' being a kingdom within heaven.

We reprise the 'Guaranteed Eternal Sanctuary Man' theme, with Hackett now on lead guitar, almost – but not quite – bending beyond the pitch of the note. Gabriel's wonderfully emotive, hoarse voice at the end closes the song as it fades off into the distance to end a triumphant epic. I remember exactly how I felt that first time I heard the piece. I felt like I'd been on a long quest, an exhausting but an exhilarating journey and I could only think of one thing: there was no need to turn the album over, the needle was going straight back to the start of 'Supper's Ready'...

Related Tracks

'Twilight Alehouse' 7:48 (Genesis)

Originally written and performed live while Phillips was still in the band, 'Twilight Alehouse' was recorded in the same sessions as *Foxtrot*. Stylistically, it does sound like an updated version of an earlier number with better production technics and a more mature vocal performance from Peter Gabriel. The song was a favourite in the live shows. There is a disparity between the verse and chorus as if they are from different songs and that limits the flow of the piece, the chorus being similar to 'Get 'em Out By Friday'. The end section works best – it is the reason that the song worked so well live with its heavier guitar and organ. Again, Banks manages to bend organ notes, by turning it on and off to slow down and speed up the tone wheels. The song was later released as the B-side to 'I Know What I Like (In Your Wardrobe)' from *Selling England by the Pound* in August 1973.

Selling England by the Pound (1973)

Personnel:
Peter Gabriel: vocals, flute, oboe, percussion
Tony Banks: keyboards, 12-string guitar
Steve Hackett: electric guitar, nylon guitar
Michael Rutherford: 12-string guitar, bass, electric sitar
Phil Collins: drums, assorted percussion, lead vocals on 'More Fool Me', backing vocals
Recorded at Island Studios, London in August 1973
Producer: Genesis with John Burns
Sleeve design: Chris Peyton. Cover painting by Betty Swanwick
Released: October 13, 1973
Label: Charisma in the UK, Atlantic in the US
Highest Chart places: UK: 3, US: 70. Achieved platinum in Canada (80,000) and gold in France (50,000), UK (100,000) and US (500,000), mostly after many years.
Running time: 53:40

As with *Nursery Cryme,* the band allocated a specific writing period for the album, taking two months out from touring and spending them in a private house in Chessington, Surrey. Rutherford remembers that the album was 'bloody hard to write', while Banks recalls it as 'depressing'. Having developed most of the previous albums during their touring schedule, performing the songs live and adapting them based on audience reaction, only a couple of ideas were brought in at the start of these writing sessions. There was a song called 'The Block' which became 'The Battle of Epping Forest' and another series of ideas from Banks that became 'Firth of Fifth'. The band found this style of writing over a fixed period difficult and initially played the two new songs they had over and over again with little inspiration for anything new. Rutherford remarks that progress was OK for the first couple of weeks, but that the next week was grim. This time pressure and the slow development of new material took its toll on several of the band, bringing about varying levels of depression, with various members thinking of leaving the band at one time or other. Banks calls it 'one of the worst times' for the band. By contrast, Gabriel remembers it as a 'relatively happy, calm period in the band's history', and Collins doesn't particularly remember it as being difficult, while Hackett recalls simply enjoying being the guitarist, contributing riffs and solos to the songs. Whatever the pressures, the resulting album is considered by many fans is the best album in the band's history.

Banks had bought his first synthesiser, an ARP Pro Soloist and used this throughout the recording, and it is particularly noticeable on the solo section of 'The Cinema Show'. He had used the Hammond organ in as many ways as he could think of, including feeding it through various effects pedals, and by this time felt he had exhausted the possibilities of the instrument.

One of the aims of the album, according to Gabriel, was to look at

'Englishness' in an oblique way and he proposed the title, Rutherford saying that it was one of the band's best album titles. This was particularly relevant as in 1973 many felt the UK was in danger of being sold to the highest bidder and there was a high awareness of the rise of commercialism. Furthermore, this was the start of a recession in both the UK and USA, triggered by an oil crisis that would last for the next two years. The situation would worsen in the following year with numerous strikes, a three-day working week in the UK and scheduled power cuts. This was also, incidentally the year that Britain, along with Denmark and Ireland, joined the European Economic Community, that would later become the European Union. Maybe now we should call this 'Brentrance'.

Interviews highlight that by this time there were tensions starting to surface within the band. The front-page popularity of Gabriel with the press, while good for the band overall, left many feeling under appreciated. Hackett says:

Pete's show tended to get reviewed, and the band didn't really get a review. It was very much he, and not they.

Collins has similar worries 'I Started to get a little bit frustrated that the people were coming to see what Peter was doing rather than hear the music' while Banks had concerns that some of the costumes had taken things a little too far, making it difficult even to get a microphone close to Gabriel's mouth at times.

The cover was a painting by Betty Swanwick who was a member of the Royal Academy. The band met up with her and had tea on her lawn to discuss the cover. She couldn't create something from scratch in the month that was available, so agreed to take an existing painting called The Dream and modify it to add the lawnmower referencing the lyrics in the single 'I Know What I Like (In Your Wardrobe)'. Gabriel described her as a 'Miss Marple' type lady even though she would only have been 58 at the time. A simple plain font was used for the Genesis logo and the title on the cover.

'Dancing With the Moonlit Knight' 8:04 (Genesis)
When performing live, Gabriel, in full Britannia costume would announce:

I am in the English Channel; it is cold, exceedingly wet. I am the voice of Britain before the Daily Express. My name is Britannia; this is my song. It is called 'Dancing with the Moonlit Knight'.

The lyrics include the pun 'knights of the green shield stamp and shout'. Green Shield stamps were given for purchases in many places in the UK during the 70s, including petrol and groceries. These were saved in a book, and once it was filled, it could be exchanged for items from a catalogue. This is the song that most captures the theme of the album, opening quietly with Gabriel's unaccompanied vocal 'Can you tell me where my country lies', then slowly building to the fast, racing section with extensive lead guitar from Hackett.

The song ends with 12 string guitar and keyboards and withers away to nothing. One of the reasons for this is that the initial intention is that this piece was going to lead into 'Cinema Show' to create a longer suite of around 20 minutes. However, the band were wary of this new song being compared to 'Supper's Ready', so decided to split the tracks up.

'I Know What I Like (In Your Wardrobe)' 4:07 (Genesis)

This short, simple track was released as a single on 3 August 1973 with 'Twilight Alehouse' as the B-side, reaching 21 in the UK charts. At one point Gabriel sings 'over the Garden Wall' which could be linked to the theme of mowing the lawn, but could also be a reference to the original band that Gabriel and Banks had formed just six years earlier. The most memorable lyric comes towards the end of the song and is referenced on the album cover,

As the sun beats down, and I lie on the bench, I can always hear them talk, Me, I'm just a lawnmower you can tell me by the way I walk.

The song opens with Gabriel proclaiming 'It's one o'clock and time for lunch, dum de dum dum'. The main character – Jacob – cuts grass for a living and sleeps on a park bench in the sun. He is being pushed to aim higher 'in the fire escape trade', but he is happy mowing lawns and says 'I know what I like, and I like what I know' highlighting that happiness doesn't always come from having the highest paid job you can achieve. The song is said to have been written about Jacob Finster who was a roadie for Genesis between 1971 and 1973. He had many jobs over the years, including mowing lawns.

Gabriel still says in interviews that he doesn't like the chorus, but the song was so popular it was played on nearly every tour including the last one in 2007 and would often incorporate short snippets of other songs from the Gabriel era.

'Firth of Fifth' 9:37 (Genesis)

Starting with a wonderful Banks piano progression in some deceptively challenging time signatures, this piece was to be a live favourite for many years. By 1977, when *Seconds Out* was recorded, Banks would drop the piano intro and the song would start with 'The path is clear' lyric. It would eventually reduce further to the end section only, played as part of a medley of older songs – something to keep fans of the early years happy. A version was even played on the *Calling All Stations* tour in 1998. Given that the lyrics contain a reference to 'a river of constant change', the title is a play on words on the estuary of the River Forth a few miles south of my own home, the Firth of Forth. The Banks synth solo, based around the opening piano section, is one of the highlights here and the song also features Hackett on what is probably the best-known Genesis guitar solo. Originally conceived by Banks as a piano and flute instrumental section, it evolved in rehearsals to include a soaring lead guitar in place of the flute.

'More Fool Me' 3:11 (Genesis)

Collins gets his second lead vocal on this short, simple ballad. Given that it was the most commercial-sounding track, it is curious that it was never released as a single, probably due to Peter Gabriel not being the lead vocalist. This was the track that many Genesis fans including myself turned to when the news emerged that Collins was to be the new voice of Genesis in 1975.

'The Battle of Epping Forest' 11:48 (Genesis)

Gabriel would keep newspaper cuttings that would interest him and one such cutting related to the gang wars in London at the time this piece was written. His cutting from *The Times* about the battle in Epping forest was accidentally misplaced, so he made up the story of two gangs fighting over protection rights in London. The original article from 5 April 1972 states:

> *One gang even challenged another to a private battle in Epping forest. Almost 50 men armed with knuckle dusters, heavy boots and razors, arrived. Combatants left the area suffering serious injuries. The winning gang, made up mainly of young men, won the concession to a protection racket in a small area of east London.*

During the song, we are introduced to fictional characters such as Willy Wright, Little John, Bob the Nob, Liquid Len and of course Mick the Prick, 'fresh out the nick'. This was another song where the instrumental backing was fully recorded before the melody and lyrics were written and added by Gabriel, making for a very busy track with lots – in fact too many – words. Collins says they were pleased with the music they had recorded, but then the lyrics came in at '300 words a line'. Lyrical clutter was almost becoming a signature sound of at least one song per album by this point, almost as if Gabriel was competing with the rest of the band in showboating their talents. In his case, it was his ability to sing as many words per bar of music as possible or indeed on this song to use as many voices as possible. It is the longest, but also one of the weaker tracks on *Selling England*.

'After the Ordeal' 4:16 (Genesis)

'After the Ordeal' is an instrumental piece written by Hackett. It opens with classical guitar and piano, followed by a hauntingly soulful electric guitar solo. The last part has twin electric guitars playing in harmony combined with Gabriel's flute, and it is beautifully melodic. Banks said at the time that the remastered edition was released, that this was the weakest track on the album and one he never felt quite comfortable with, although perhaps this is down to his own piano performance which does feel overly complicated.

'The Cinema Show' 11:05 (Genesis)

The lyrics for this track are in two distinct sections. The first tells of a modern-day Romeo and Juliet preparing for a date, and in another classical reference, the second tells of Father Tiresias. Tiresias was a soothsayer, a prophet who is said to have been blinded by the gods because he told their secrets to mortals. He was transformed into a woman for seven years by Hera after striking two copulating snakes with his stick. 'Once a man, like the sea I raged. Once a woman, like the earth I gave.' He was called before the Gods to tell them who enjoyed sex more, the man or the woman.

The dual 12-String guitars of Rutherford and Banks weave beautifully around each other in the first part of the song, once again in a long-forgotten tuning, followed by the faster section in 7/8 with what is undoubtedly the best, and the longest solo of Banks' career at almost six minutes, played on his ARP Pro-soloist synthesiser. Like many fans of Genesis from that era, I know that solo note for note and love every one of them. It's a classic.

'Aisle of Plenty' 1:32 (Genesis)

The album ends with another commentary on commercialisation, bookending the album after 'Dancing with the Moonlit Knight'. The 'aisles' being those in a supermarket, shelves piled high. The lyrics are laden with retail-orientated puns, likely only understood by those familiar with UK supermarkets in the early 1970s. 'Easy now, there's the safe way home. Thankful for her fine fare discounts, Tess co-operates', referring to Safeway, Fine Fare, Tesco and The Co-Operative Society, respectively. Safeway and Fine Fare, sadly, are long gone.

The Lamb Lies Down on Broadway (1974)

Personnel:
Peter Gabriel: lead vocals, flute, varied instruments, 'experiments with foreign sounds'
Steve Hackett: acoustic and electric guitars
Mike Rutherford: bass guitar, 12-string guitar
Tony Banks: Hammond T-102 organ, RMI 368x Electra Piano and Harpsichord, Mellotron M-400, ARP Pro Soloist synthesiser, Elka Rhapsody string synthesiser, piano
Phil Collins: drums, percussion, vibraphone, backing vocals, second lead vocal on 'The Colony of Slippermen'
Brian Eno: Enossification (vocal treatments) on 'In the Cage' and 'The Grand Parade of Lifeless Packaging'
Recorded at Glaspant Manor, Carmarthenshire Wales using the Island Studios mobile unit between August and October 1974
Producer: Genesis with John Burns
Sleeve design: Hipgnosis
Released: November 18, 1974
Label: Charisma in the UK, ATCO in the US
Highest Chart places: UK: 10, US: 41. Achieved gold in France (50,000), UK (100,000) and US (500,000).
Running time: 94:12

The Lamb Lies Down On Broadway stands as the pinnacle of the Gabriel era, regarded by him as one of the two high points of his career with Genesis, the other being 'Supper's Ready'. Collins also says that the album was the best music they created and remains his favourite with the band. It is – arguably – one of the defining classics both of the progressive rock genre and rock theatre.

The band took a different approach to the writing of the album, having previously worked in groups of two or more, with the lyric writing shared. After his experience with 'Supper's Ready', Gabriel wanted to write all the lyrics and tell a complete story, with the rest of the band writing the music, often through jam sessions. He also proposed the idea that was to become the album concept. Another idea on the table at the time was a proposal from Rutherford to write a story based on The Little Prince by Antoine de Saint-Exupéry, but this was viewed by the rest of the band as a bit 'twee'. It had already been decided to record a double album in order to allow more freedom for the music, letting it breathe and one of the possibilities was to split the album into two separate releases six months apart. This didn't happen, but it would certainly have given more time to write the lyrics and work on the music, as the album was completed in a mad rush at the last minute. Double albums were the 'in thing' at the time, Yes having released Tales From Topographic Oceans six month earlier and Elton John's Goodbye Yellow Brick Road had been released the previous year. Led Zeppelin would release Physical Graffiti in 1975.

In June 1974 the band moved into Headley Grange in East Hampshire for three months to develop the concept, finding the house in a very poor condition, having been used previously by Bad Company and Led Zeppelin. Robert Plant told Hackett later that he was sure the place was haunted, while Collins vividly describes how there were rats inside the house at the time, wandering the hallways oblivious to the new human occupants. The recording itself was later made at Glaspant Manor in Wales using the mobile recording unit from Island studios.

Lyric writing was clearly a source of tension in the band. In a later interview, Gabriel recalls with a smile on his face that the main writer of each song would come to him to 'discuss the lyrics', but he wasn't about to give up his control over the word content. Banks and Rutherford have also mentioned that they were frustrated that they had little input into the lyrics of the music they were writing.

During the time at Headley Grange, Gabriel was offered work on a screenplay by William Friedkin, who had directed *The Exorcist* in 1973. Friedkin had read the short story on the back of *Genesis Live* and thought that Gabriel had an 'interesting mind'. Gabriel was given an ultimatum to choose between the band and Friedkin. He chose to leave and pursue the opportunity with the director. The band weren't sure if he had really left or if he would return, so they continued to write with Rutherford commenting that during this period they decided that they would carry on as a band without a singer and record an instrumental album if necessary. However, within a week, Gabriel returned as the work with Friedkin came to nothing.

Tensions within the band were growing, and Gabriel was often separated from the others, spending most of his time upstairs writing lyrics while the band wrote the music downstairs. Gabriel's wife Jill also suffered a complicated birth of their first Daughter Anna-Marie on 26 July 1974. She contracted an infection from the epidural needle, and their daughter was in an incubator after the umbilical cord had been wrapped around the neck during birth. Unsure if she would survive for the first couple of weeks, Gabriel, quite understandably, wanted to spend time with both of them and travelled back to London to be with them on a regular basis. Thankfully, all worked out well for Anna-Marie Gabriel who would go on to become a film director and would direct two DVDs for her father, *Growing Up on Tour: A Family Portrait* and *Still Growing Up: Live & Unwrapped*. Both Banks and Rutherford admitted later that they were 'horribly unsupportive' of Gabriel during this period, as nobody else in the band had yet had children. Gabriel remembers that his need to be with his family was taken as a lack of interest and involvement in the band which made him quite angry. Collins says, 'at that time there was only the band or not the band' nothing else. Hackett was also in the middle of the breakup of his first marriage to Ellen Busse, so with all those tensions, getting away in secluded isolation as a band to write ended up not being the creative environment it was expected to be.

The album loosely tells a story of Rael, a Puerto Rican immigrant living in

New York City, who finds himself in some form of the underworld, searching for a way out. The story is also used as a metaphor for someone searching for themselves and for some form of salvation. The story is somewhat vague, and even the album synopsis sheds only a little light on the actual – or implied – meanings. Several of the themes clearly come from Gabriel's own inner demons, that he felt trapped and limited within the band and was looking for a way out. Gabriel later cited his influences as West Side Story, 'a kind of punk' Pilgrim's Progress, the works of Carl Jung and the film El Topo, directed by Alejandro Jodorowsky who would later work with Gabriel on a screenplay for the story. The narrative follows the typical 'hero's journey', the monomyth template as described by Joseph Campbell in his book The Hero with a Thousand Faces, used in countless books and movies. Consider A Pilgrim's Progress, Moby Dick, The Hobbit, Lord of The Rings, Star Wars and of course Gabriel's inspiration, El Topo, as examples. In his book, Campbell describes the 'hero's journey' in several stages. First, he or she is called upon to undertake an adventure, often reluctantly, then passes from a familiar to an unfamiliar environment where they meet a mentor or helper figure. Next, they undergo a series of challenges or tests until they reach some form of revelation which results in a transformation or enlightenment before finally returning to their known world. Think of Frodo and Gandalf or Luke Skywalker and Obi-Wan Kenobi as the hero and helper figures.

Brian Eno is credited with so-called 'Enossification' in the sleeve notes. He was working in the studio upstairs at Island in London when The Lamb was being mixed so Gabriel had him add some vocal effects. Banks remembers it being such a tiny contribution, that he has no idea why they credited Eno on the sleeve. Collins was sent upstairs to record drums on a track on Eno's album Taking Tiger Mountain By Strategy, as a trade.

The subsequent tour of the US started just two days after the release of the album, kicking off in Chicago on 20 November 1974. The elaborate stage shows used props, costumes, lasers and three large screens behind the band, where 1,450 slides would be projected with varying degrees of success each night. Early in the tour, Gabriel decided he had enough and announced that he wanted to leave the band. He recalls telling the others and says: 'It was like telling someone that you had decided to kill their child, not a good feeling.'

Manager Tony Smith remembers that during the first week of the American tour, Gabriel came to him to break the news that he was leaving. Banks tried to talk him out of it as he was his friend, but also because he didn't know if the band could survive without him. With almost six months of dates already booked for the promotional tour, Gabriel agreed to continue, ending with his last performance in Besançon, France on 22 May 1975. Gabriel played the 'Last Post' on the oboe backstage before the gig. The news broke in *The Melody Maker* on 16 August with the headline 'Gabriel Out of Genesis?', although no formal statement had been made over the preceding nine months since Gabriel's decision to leave.

The sleeve design was the first of four from Hipgnosis, the London based design company run by Storm Thorgerson, and Aubrey Powell, aka Po. They had designed many of the now iconic album covers of the time including *Dark Side Of The Moon* for Pink Floyd and *Houses Of The Holy* for Led Zeppelin. The front sleeve depicts scenes from the story, with Rael portrayed by a model credited as 'Omar' in the Steve notes. Gabriel wasn't happy with the choice of the actor as he clearly envisaged the character as Puerto Rican. It was also the first cover to use the angular Genesis logo that the band would return to for *Second's Out* and *...and then there were three...*.

Given that it is a concept album, the track information has been organised here as a short description of the storyline, with comments on lyrical references followed by comments on the musical content. I have tried to avoid going into too deep a dive into the lyrical meanings. There are many social, sexual, classical and religious references in the words, but while Gabriel pulled information from many sources to write his often very clever lyrics, he regularly wrote words that simply sounded good when sung together, so not every line should be expected to make sense.

Album one, side one
'The Lamb Lies Down on Broadway' 4:52 (Genesis)
Early one morning, Rael, a half Puerto Rican punk from the streets emerges out of the New York subway, spray paint can in his hand, having left his mark on the walls underground. Full of aggression and attitude, he is mesmerised by the strangest of things, a lamb that lies down on Broadway. Initially, he can't think what it means until he realises that this may be a symbol of his impending death.

Starting quietly, with Banks playing double handed piano chords, the introduction builds much like an overture at the theatre. The track is driven by Rutherford's punching, aggressive bass line and Collins' superb drumming. Gabriel sings the part of Rael with attitude and aggression, describing the drug stores opening in the morning, addicts coming down from their highs and endless cars travelling through the city. Rael knows something is about to happen when he says 'Something inside me has just begun. Lord knows what I have done'. Even in this relatively short, introductory song, we have a quiet interlude at 2:30 as Real sees the lamb for the first time. The end of the song quotes 'On Broadway' by the Drifters, 'They say the lights are always bright on Broadway. On Broadway. They say there's always magic in the air'.

'Fly on a Windshield' 2:47 (Genesis)
While still wondering what the lamb might mean, Real sees a huge dark cloud descend upon Times Square, turning solid and morphing into a wall, but only Rael seems to be able to see it, everyone else 'carries on as if nothing was there'. Rael tries to run from the danger, but a wind starts up and blows dust

over him until he feels like he is hovering, covered in a crust of dust, unable to move, waiting to die, like a fly waiting to be hit by a windshield.

A quiet Mellotron and a single guitar strums, mirroring the quiet confusion of Rael, then Gabriel forms the imagery of the cloud in Times Square, which looks like it is descending, and as he is hovering, BANG we are into the heartbeat rhythms of the desert inspired instrumental section complete with some superb, wailing Hackett guitar. This is the first of the many musical sections written through improvisation and jam sessions and one of my favourites. Banks' chord sequence and Mellotron sound evoke an image of a desert with camels slowly moving across it. Rutherford called it 'Pharaohs going down the Nile', and the piece rises and builds with drama ready for the next track which follows seamlessly.

'Broadway Melody of 1974' 2:11 (Genesis)

There were a series of four *Broadway Melody of ....* movies, released in 1929, 1936, 1938 and 1940, which influenced the title of this song. All four movies tell, essentially, the story of a group of people 'putting on a show'. Images of New York and American life flash through Rael's mind: Lenny Bruce, the Ku Klux Klan, Groucho Marx, Caryl Chessman, Howard Hughes and Winston cigarettes to name a few. After the lyrics on the previous album had drawn criticism for being particularly 'English', Gabriel wanted to get away from this with 'The Lamb', and this track, in particular, showed a broadening of influences via its lyrical content and cultural references. In 1974 there was no internet, no easy way to find information other than a library, buying books or talking with others, and yet Gabriel manages to include numerous, often obscure references throughout the song. In the genesis of a few years ago, many of these would have been from mythological and religious sources, but here we have many American social references. As an example, take the lines 'The cheerleader waves her cyanide wand, there's a smell of peach blossom and bitter almond. Caryl Chessman sniffs the air and leads the parade; he knows in a scent you can bottle all you made'. Caryl Chessman was a serial criminal who was convicted on seventeen counts of abduction, theft and rape in Los Angeles in 1948. After eight stays of execution by the state of California, he held the record for the longest stay on death row at twelve years by the time of his execution. The cyanide wand possibly references the execution, cyanide smelling like bitter almond. All of this appears in a couple of lines of one song – quite amazing.

After the pomp and intricate instrumental ending to 'Fly On A Windshield', this song uses a much simpler, driving beat to provide the backing for Gabriel's essay on American life. The end of the song quietens, as Rael falls asleep.

'Cuckoo Cocoon' 2:14 (Genesis)

Awakening in a cave surrounded by some form of 'powdered wool' not knowing if he is in some comfortable jail in Brooklyn or is Jonah inside the whale, Rael wonders if he has woken too soon. The line 'Cuckoo Cocoon, have I come to, too soon for you' is interesting, he feels lost, out of place and wrapped up, hence the 'Cuckoo Cocoon', but he thinks he has awoken too early, 'Have I come to, too soon for you'. Eventually, Rael falls back asleep.

The tension and mystery of the opening three songs are broken by a gentle, almost folky arrangement for guitar and piano with a soft, fluttering flute solo from Gabriel through its second half. It forms a comforting contrast to the earlier pieces and mirrors Rael's emotional state at this time.

'In the Cage' 8:15 (Genesis)

Rael awakes once again to find himself enclosed in a cage formed by stalactites, (the ones that come down), and stalagmites, (the ones that go up). He sees his brother John fleetingly outside the cage, but John doesn't seem to see Rael and disappears when Rael tries to call out to him for help. Many commentators speculate that both Rael and John were drug addicts and that John had died from an overdose, leaving Rael with a significant amount of guilt. Nothing in the lyrics, the album cover story or any insight from Gabriel support this, although given the vagueness of the overall story, so much is left to the imagination of the listener that this interpretation is quite possible.

From the quieter interlude of 'Cuckoo Cocoon,' we are once again back to a familiar driving heartbeat rhythm, mirroring the fear and urgency felt by Rael at his latest predicament. The rhythm and tempo increase as Rael realises he is trapped and panic sets in. The music changes character again as Rael sees a possible way out. We are treated to the first Banks synth solo of the album halfway through the song before Rael sees John outside the cage accompanied by an almost discordant section, then we are once again into the galloping verse. This the first time we hear the vocal treatments from Eno, feeding the voice through a synthesiser to distort and change the pitch and timbre of the voice. Once the main song has faded, there is an electronic interlude.

This track would remain a favourite for live shows for many years and would become part of a medley of older songs, right up until the 2007 reunion tour.

'The Grand Parade of Lifeless Packaging' 2:45 (Genesis)

The next ordeal finds Rael in some form of factory where lifeless humans are packaged up and shipped off to some unknown fate. Once again, he sees John. It isn't clear if John is part of the workers on the production line at number nine or is part of the merchandise. Given the overall flow of the underlying story, I expect Rael is being packaged the same way as John, so Rael is retracing a journey that John has already taken previously, supporting the notion that they have both descended into a drug-induced decline.

The announcement at the beginning of the song 'It's the last great adventure left to mankind, screams a drooping lady offering her dream dolls at less than extortionate prices'. Many writers refer to death as the 'last great adventure'.

The song features a strong marching beat that builds in urgency through the length of the piece, becoming almost manic at one point, emphasising the clockwork nature of the grand parade before it breaks into a different beat with 'The halls run like clockwork'. This provides temporary relief before a return to the solid marching beat. This song is the second track to feature Eno's distinctive vocal treatment work, which is used as the song draws to a close and the tempo slows as if the mechanical aspects of the factory are slowly grinding to a halt, bringing the first side of original LP to a close.

Album one, side two
'Back in N.Y.C.' 5:49 (Genesis)
Rael experiences either a flashback to New York, or some form of New York recreated in his new underworld home. He is instantly on the offensive to prove his status on the street, referencing his stay at Pontiac juvenile correct centre. This song gives the strongest hint of drug abuse so far in the line 'who needs illusion of love and affection when you are walking in the streets with your mainline connection'. This is an idea further reinforced as the imagery become increasingly surreal as if Rael is in a drug-induced state, no more so than when he finds himself cuddling a porcupine and holding his hairy heart realising, of the hair, that it is 'time to shave it off'.

The ever-present bass heartbeat kicks off the second side of the first record with the lyric 'I see faces and traces of home, back In New York City' announcing that Rael is – possibly – back home. A pounding rhythm and relentless synthesiser arpeggio from Banks drive the track forward. Once again Rael is in his home town, and his aggression level rises again as Gabriel almost rasps and snarls some of the lyrics. Collins' drumming is outstanding on this song creating a complex rhythm that helps accentuate the urgency of the situation Rael finds himself in.

'Hairless Heart' 2:25 (Genesis)
Left with his heart shaved of hair, his soul exposed, Rael is left to reflect on his journey so far as a beautiful sound surrounds him. This is very much a Hackett composition, complete with fingerstyle classical guitar and his signature volume pedal swell from his lead guitar. Banks plays light organ arpeggios under the guitars, then comes in with this beautiful solo melody in the middle. This beautiful track brings us down from the high energy of the previous song.

'Counting Out Time' 3:45 (Genesis)
Another memory comes to Rael, about a time when he purchased a book on sex 'Erogenous Zones and Difficulties in Overcoming Finding Them', after finding a girl he wanted to date. This is quite a whimsical interlude – very much out of context within the storyline – but it provides light relief, allowing the listener to relax for a few minutes. It was written by Gabriel and parallels 'Willow Farm' on 'Supper's Ready' as a song inserted part way through a longer

piece to break the tension. It was released as a single, even though the lyrics were quite risqué and full of innuendo, referencing masturbation: 'Without you, mankind handkinds through the blues'.

The guitar solo is played using an EMS Synthi Hi Fli guitar synthesiser to produce a sound similar to a Stylophone (a handheld electronic instrument popular in the 1970s) which I can only describe as 'squidgy'. The song was released as the first of two singles from the album on 1 November 1974, with 'Riding The Scree' as the B-side, though it didn't chart.

'The Carpet Crawlers' 5:16 (Genesis)

Rael finds himself crawling on a soft floor like lambswool with many others, all heading in the same direction through a red ochre corridor towards a heavy wooden door. It seems the nearer the door they get, the more lifeblood they appear to have. The refrain of 'We've got to get in to get out' implying that only through the door lies a way out of this underworld.

A beautiful and comforting ballad, the song mirrors the relative safety and comfort Rael is feeling. It is more evident on the chorus of this song than any other how frequently Gabriel and Collins sing together throughout the album. It was the second single to be released, in April 1975 with a B-side taken from a live version of 'The Waiting Room' using its work in progress title 'The Waiting Room (Evil Jam)', but again it failed to chart. A new version was recorded in 1999 for the *Turn It On Again: The Hits* release titled 'The Carpet Crawlers 1999,'with both Gabriel and Collins providing lead vocals.

'The Chamber of 32 Doors' 5:40 (Genesis)

Through the door lies a complex choice, more difficult than a simple crossroads. Rael is presented by a chamber with, yes, 32 doors through which he can choose to exit. Hundreds of others are also in the room trying to work out how to get out. As Rael tries many of the doors, he finds himself back again in the chamber. Surrounded by people from every walk of life, all having the same struggle, Rael starts to lose hope, offering up all his dreams for a way out.

This is the song which most reflects how Gabriel was feeling at this point. It was added late in the writing process after he returned from the time spent with Friedkin and tells of someone who is looking at their choices in life and finding no matter what they decide, or how they try to change direction, nothing is different, and that they are right back where they started. It is summed up in the last lines 'I've nowhere, nowhere to hide, I'd give you all of my dreams if you'd help me find a door that doesn't lead me back again. Take me away'.

This is a low point emotionally and physically. Until now, Rael has been descending into the underground, but now he starts to rise with the spiral staircase leading up to the chamber. Being the end of the first vinyl album, the song cleanly separates the story into two parts – the first of descent and decline, and the second of rebirth, recovery, rising and salvation.

Hackett opens with a wonderfully mournful solo over Mellotron and bass pedals before 'At the top of the stairs' brings us back to the storyline. The song has a very soul-orientated melody, referencing Gabriel's early musical preferences. The music is pared back to piano for the last few bars, and Gabriel's vocal is beautifully soulful, sounding almost broken by the end, which adds so much to this song's theme of despair.

Album two, side one
'Lilywhite Lilith' 2:40 (Genesis)

Having almost lost all hope, Rael hears a voice in the crowd asking for help. It is a blind woman – Lilywhite Lilith – offering to help Rael find a way out if he, in turn, helps her. She leads him through a tunnel of light to a large round cave where he is placed upon a cold jade throne. Telling Rael that 'they' are coming for him and not to be afraid, she leaves as two golden globes float into the room. On each of the four sides, an upbeat song is chosen to open a new side of the album. The song had already been played at gigs from 1971 under the name 'The Light', and a performance from March 1971 in Belgium is available online.

Based around a repeated, rising guitar and bass run, the song includes extensive high register backing vocals from Gabriel and Collins in the chorus, while Hackett provides some excellent guitar throughout.

'The Waiting Room' 5:28 (Genesis)

Rael waits for whatever fate will befall him.

This is one of the stranger pieces on the album, deriving from one of the band's many jams. This one was originally being called 'The Evil Jam,' complete with strange noises and sound effects. At times it sounds like a combination of cats meowing and aircraft dive-bombing. Collins recalls how they were making some 'really nasty sounds' while it was raining outside, before moving to a more melodic mood which lifts the tension and ends the track in a harmonious and lighter mode, by which time the sun had come out, and there was a rainbow in the sky. Like many, I'm not a big fan of the first section but the second half is superb. It works really well because it builds a structure out of the chaos and discord of the first section.

When the album was released, I went to my local record store where there were listening booths about the size of an old public telephone box. You could get a couple of people in each – three at a squeeze. Each booth was linked to a turntable at the counter. I had heard a couple of tracks from the album on John Peel's show already, but for some reason, the second LP was put on, and we heard 'Lilywhite Lilith' and 'The Waiting Room'. I remember my friend declaring 'this is pretty rubbish', when faced with the Avant-Garde nature of the second track, but there was no doubt in my mind. I was buying it anyway.

'Anyway' 3:18 (Genesis)

While waiting, Rael contemplates his death, referencing the body returning to the soil. He is brought out of his reverie by a voice apologising for the wait and telling him that it 'won't be long'.

This song is another personal favourite, with great lyrics featuring multiple references to death. Gabriel's delivery on this song is inspired, with 'It's getting hard to catch my breath' speeded up toward the end of the song running the words together as if he is breathless and 'back to ash' is sung as 'sbacktoash' without a pause. This song had been around for a while, and a version of it called 'Frustration' was recorded for a BBC documentary about the painter Michael Jackson that never aired.

That metronomic motif which runs through the album is back for this song as we start out with piano chord arpeggios from Banks in a relaxed mood, as Rael is philosophical about his end. However, the latter part of the song doubles in tempo as Rael is told he won't have long to wait. Hackett's harmony guitar plays a big part in the middle section before the final verse and the slow strings that end the song.

'Here Comes The Supernatural Anaesthetist' 2:50 (Genesis)

Death appears to Rael in the form of the Supernatural Anaesthetist which seems like a throwback to the Guaranteed Eternal Sanctuary Man in 'Supper's Ready'. 'If he wants you to snuff it, all he has to do is puff it', and apparently, he is 'such a fine dancer'.

Apart from the short lyrical introduction to the Supernatural Anaesthetist, this is an instrumental with a guitar solo that always reminds me of a bizarre dance, probably influenced by the line about death being such 'a fine dancer.' The end of the piece shifts to dramatic Mellotron chords with further great guitar work and finally some eerie, reversed chimes as if, once again, Rael is falling into unconsciousness.

'The Lamia' 6:57 (Genesis)

Rael follows a scent down a long passageway, lit by chandeliers and finds a rose-water pool covered in mist. Seeing movement in the water, he realises he isn't alone and sees a vision of beauty emerge from the pool in the form of three snakes with female faces. This entrances him, their every movement filled with grace. The Lamia welcome Rael and invite him to enter. He undresses and slips into the pool, their tongues tasting his body as he has a sexual encounter with the three beings. As their fangs draw blood, their faces contort, and they die saying 'we all have loved you, Rael'. Rael holds the limp bodies of the Lamia and decides for some strange reason to eat the flesh before leaving, just as they had planned to eat his.

As in many earlier songs, Greek mythology is, once again, referenced here. Lamia was a mistress of Zeus, but his wife Hera became angry and jealous of her, killing her children and transforming her into a child-eating monster. Hera also cursed Lamia with permanent insomnia so she would be in constant sorrow, but Zeus provided her with the ability to remove her eyes. The story is recounted in the John Keats poem 'Lamia' written in 1819. Later tales of Lamia added the serpent-like properties, or a half snake, half woman creature who would lure young men to satisfy their sexual desires and then feed on the flesh of their victims afterwards.

There are serenity and calm about this song, and given the point in the story, I always felt like this was a second low point for Rael. Even though he is loved by the Lamia he does this knowing that he has no other option, and as he is waiting for death, he has resigned himself to whatever fate awaits him. He has little fight left.

Along with 'Carpet Crawlers', this is one of the most beautiful tracks on the album. Drums are used sparingly as the track ebbs and flows like both the water in the pool and the bodies of the writhing Lamia. A lovely piano solo in the middle section gives way to a Mellotron choir and falls back again to a quiet synthesiser solo before ending on a flute and guitar section that oozes sadness.

'Silent Sorrow in Empty Boats' 3:06 (Genesis)
The limp bodies of The Lamia are described by Rael as 'Silent Sorrows in Empty Boats'. This is a melancholic piece centred around Hackett's lead guitar combined with other treated guitar and keyboard textures. Once again, we also have a wonderful Mellotron choir which provides a fitting anthem with which to mourn the Lamia.

Album two, side two
'The Colony of Slippermen (The Arrival – A Visit to the Doktor – The Raven)' 8:14 (Genesis)
Having eaten the bodies of The Lamia, Rael awakes again amongst grotesque creatures, the Slippermen, who have all had the same experience as Rael with the Lamia and now their heads have swollen, their bodies covered in large lumps or bubbles. At this point in the live performance, Gabriel would wear a large costume complete with inflatable body parts. Calling it 'The Colony', combined with the transformation of their bodies suggest a parallel with a leper colony. Rael is shocked to find that he now looks the same and has himself become a Slipperman. Once again, he finds that his brother John is here, he too has become a Slipperman. John explains that the only way to 'cure' their condition is to be castrated, so they go to meet Doktor Dyper who whips off their manhood in an attempt to cure them. Their penises are placed in yellow tubes to be worn around their necks, but as the Doktor places Rael's 'windscreen wiper' into a tube, a raven swoops and picks it up, flying off. When asked for help once more, John again refuses and walks away.

The first section 'The Arrival' contains more of 'The Waiting Room' style noises – this time like monkeys in the jungle – with a Japanese Koto paying over the top. I generally wait through this for the relief of the 'Bobbity bop' and the quote from Wordsworth 'I wandered lonely as a cloud', to open the middle section and the visit to the doctor. For the first time in several songs, the music is more positive, mirroring Rael finding some fight again and seeing a potential way out of his predicament. Banks carries the song with an interesting chord pattern augmented by Hackett's guitar. Gabriel emulates the Slippermen at one part in a rasping low, throaty voice that is more effective than the Enossification used elsewhere. The second part has Banks again providing a synth solo, elevated with the arrival of the organ towards the end. The solo would find a place in an 'old medley' in later live shows, in another song where Collins' vocal backing is very apparent.

'Ravine' 2:05 (Genesis)

As the raven flies off with Rael in hot pursuit, it drops the tube into the fast-flowing rapids at the bottom of the ravine. It isn't clear how the story moves from the cave of the Slippermen to the outdoors and the ravine. A mixture of white noise 'wind' and high-pitched synthesiser, work well to conjure the image of being up on a high, windy ridge looking down on a ravine. What sounds like a treated guitar adds a chanting effect to the piece but overall this is one of the less interesting tracks that could likely have been omitted without any loss to the album overall.

'The Light Dies Down on Broadway' 3:32 (Genesis)

As Rael heads off to retrieve his yellow plastic 'shoobedoobe', he sees a glimpse of New York through a window in the bank as if there is an opportunity to escape this nightmare. As he contemplates whether to head for the vision, he hears John cry for help from the water and decides to go after him. The vision fades as 'The Light Dies Down on Broadway'. John has appeared three times before this in the story, and has walked away, first was when he was in the cage, then when he was in the grand parade of lifeless packaging and finally when at the Doktor's. Perhaps this is a veiled reference to the 'Gospels' when Jesus predicted that Peter would deny him three times before the cock crowed in the morning, but would ultimately be forgiven for it. If this is the case, the raven could possibly be the cock, and Rael's forgiveness is shown by his decision to plunge into the rapids to save John.

The track was another of the gaps left during writing that was filled late in the recording with lyrics that weren't written by Gabriel. It is a reprise of the first track on the album with a simple replacement of 'light dies' for 'lamb lies' when the option of escape and the image of home fades. The other notable change is the aggression of the territorial declaration in the line 'I'm Rael' is replaced by an almost plaintive, desperate plea, 'My home'.

Another favourite of mine, this version, in many ways, is better than the opening track. However, Rael is much more humble, having lost his aggression after castration. Gabriel sings in a rather more mellow, even melancholic tone, losing the rasp and aggression used in the earlier song.

'Riding the Scree' 3:56 (Genesis)

Scrambling down the loose, broken rocks at the side of the Ravine, Rael realises he must ditch his fears and take a dive if he is to save John, saying 'Evel Knievel you got nothing on me'. Evel Knievel was a US daredevil who attempted to jump over the Snake River Canyon in southern Idaho on a steam-powered rocket in September 1974, which was during the middle of recording the album.

The first half of the track uses a halting, start-stop staccato rhythm on drums, bass and guitar with a great 'Cinema Show-esque' solo from Banks with diving pitch bent notes at times indicative of Rael's fall down the loose gravel of the banking. The main synth line sounds almost like a version of 'El Jarabe Tapatio,' the Mexican Hat Dance. The rhythm carries on as Gabriel describes the journey down the slope to save John.

'In the Rapids' 2:24 (Genesis)

Pulled along by the strong currents and disorientated by the undertow, Rael finds he has somehow got ahead of John and hangs onto a rock to wait for his brother to pass. He grabs John and holds him tight, relieved to know they will both escape this terror, but as he looks at his brother, what he sees that it not John, but his own face. There are several more references to death here and the passing over from one side to another. 'In the cold, feel the cold all around', 'Striking out to reach you, I can't get to the other side' and as he believes he has escaped 'The dark and deep have no-one left to keep'.

In contrast to the raging rapids that, Rael is being carried through we have a light paced, slowly building piece with some superb guitar work. This leaves me with the impression that despite the fast-moving pace of the physical world of Rael in the rapids, he has lost all hope once again, and is drifting away into unconsciousness, and possibly death. The pace only picks up again at the point he manages to grab John as he floats past and sings 'Something's changed, that's not your face, It's mine. It's mine!'.

'It' 4:14 (Genesis)

The difference between Rael and the John blurs until they become fluid and melt into the purple haze that has formed around them and he becomes at one with everything around him, like the Star Child at the end of *2001: A Space Odyssey*. Even in this last song, we have more drug references such as 'When you ride the horse without a hoof' – the horse with no hooves being another name for heroin. A reference is also made to the Rolling Stones with the pun 'It's only knock and know all, but I like it'. There is even a tongue in cheek reference to progressive rock movement in 'If you think that it's pretentious, you've been taken for a ride'. Let's face it, what could be more pretentious and self-indulgent that a double album that tells a surreal story of the underworld. 'It' is one of the simplest and most upbeat tracks on the album, and it almost seems out of place as the song tries to sum up the concept of 'It' and the final elation of Rael.

Starting with a rising synthesiser tone and strummed guitar riff, this high-speed end to the album, while somewhat out of keeping with the rest of the music, has every member of the band playing on top form. The bass and drumming are amongst the best and fastest on the album with guitar and synthesiser playing the main riff through the second half of the piece as it fades away.

If the 23 minutes of 'Supper's Ready' left me feeling like I'd just listened to something very special, then this album had an even bigger impact on me. It is probably my favourite of all progressive rock albums and a piece of music that has kept me looking in the faint hope that I'll discover another equally wonderful album at some point. I've come close a few times, but I have never found an album that makes me feel the same way as this one does. The advent of CDs and the eventual loss of the vinyl album format, with its large gatefold sleeve containing notes and lyrics, allowing me to read along with each track, took away a big part of the experience. Even with the return of vinyl, most modern vinyl sleeves are culled from the CD design with all their size constraints. It is even worse to contemplate that many will hear this album for the first, and possibly the last time, on a streaming service without any notes or lyrics in their hands.

Related tracks:
Given the band had to write some last-minute pieces to fill in some gaps, there are no known additional tracks left off the release. Indeed we have already noted that the band were bringing in unused material from as far back as 1970 and 1971 to complete the album.

'Frustration' 3:42 (Genesis)
Recorded as part of a set of songs for a BBC documentary in 1970 about painter Michael Jackson which was never broadcast, this was to become 'Anyway' four years later. Much of what is recorded here was retained on *The Lamb Lies Down On Broadway,* from the piano arpeggios to the use of the word 'anyway' at the start of each line, although the other lyrical content would change. The faster piano part in the middle of the song was also retained, and only the end was discarded. It was released on the *Genesis 1970-1975* box set.

'The Light' 8:49 (Genesis)
No studio recording of 'The Light' has been released to date, though there is a poor-quality YouTube audio only version recorded live in Belgium in 1971. The opening part would become 'Lillywhite Lilith' with little change to the verse, retaining the melody and the drum phrasing, but paired with a new chorus.

'The Carpet Crawlers 1999' 5:39 (Genesis)
This is a re-worked, modern take on the composition 25 years after it was

written, produced by famed producer Trevor Horn. Hackett and Gabriel returned to record this version for the *Turn It On Again – The Hits* album and both Gabriel and Collins sing lead vocals on this, which promises much, given Horn's pedigree as a producer, but this version doesn't really make any improvements on this classic Genesis song. The fifth verse where the original begins 'The porcelain mannequin fears attack' is not used, the band choosing to keep with the slow warm feeling of the earlier part of the song, so we miss out on the wonderful line 'And the tickler takes his tickle back (stickleback)'. This was the last studio recording ever made by the band, and it is fitting that every member of the classic five-person line up were involved in it. It was released as a single in 1999 with 'Follow You Follow Me' from *...and then there were three...* and 'Turn It On Again' from *Duke* as B-sides.

A Trick of the Tail (1976)

Personnel:
Mike Rutherford: 12-string guitar, bass, bass pedals
Tony Banks: pianos, synthesisers, organ, Mellotron, 12-string guitar, backing vocals
Phil Collins: drums, percussion, lead & backing vocals
Steve Hackett: electric guitar, 12-string guitars
Recorded at Trident Studios. London between October and November 1975
Producer: David Hentschel and Genesis
Sleeve design: Hipgnosis
Released: February 2, 1976
Label: Charisma, Atco
Highest Chart places: UK: 3, US: 31. Achieved gold in France (50,000), UK (100,000) and US (500,000).
Running time: 51:08

After Gabriel's decision to leave at the end of the *Lamb* tour, the future of the band was once again in question. The news was kept from the press while the band decided what to do next, all along still hoping Gabriel would reconsider and return. Hackett concentrated on his first solo album *Voyage of the Acolyte*, which involved both Rutherford and Collins, unsure whether another Genesis release was on the horizon. The band gathered in July 1975 to work on new material while continuing the search for a replacement vocalist. Banks brought some songs he had originally worked on for a solo project which formed the starting point for *A Trick of the Tail*. It was at this time that the (in)famous *Melody Maker* advert appeared, asking for a 'singer for a Genesis-type group', which reputedly received around 400 replies. Singers were auditioned every Monday, with the management whittling down tapes and sending them to the band for selection. Banks remembers listening to 40 or 50 tapes and auditioning around twelve of the singers. In August, *Melody Maker* broke the news of Gabriel's departure and declared the group dead, forcing the band to deny any split and claim they had a new album ready to record.

By October, the recording was due to begin, and no lead singer had been found. Collins believed that they could continue as an instrumental group, but the other three felt that their music would be too dull without vocals. Recording began with the aim of working on the instrumental parts while continuing their search. Of the 400 or applicants, one singer – Mick Strickland – was brought into the studio to see how things would work out, but in the end, the tracks weren't in the right key for his voice. Banks has said that he felt that with Collins' 'lovely soft voice', he could sing the quieter songs like 'Mad Man Moon' and 'Ripples' but didn't think he would want to take on the role of lead vocalist. However, Collins was having to train the prospective singers for auditions and was finding the process frustrating. Eventually, it was decided to have Collins try out one of the louder songs, which was 'Squonk', and in the words of producer David Hentschel, 'it worked out great'. The vocals for the other tracks were then recorded in quick succession. Once complete, the band continued to look for a singer to take on the road with them, though Collins says that by this time it was a half-hearted attempt, as they realised they were going to have the same issues they had with their previous search. In the end, it was Collins' first wife who first suggested he go ahead and sing on the tour. I remember vividly when the news broke that Collins would sing lead, like many other Genesis fans, I reached for *Selling England By The Pound* to listen to 'More Fool Me', having never really noticed it wasn't Gabriel singing that song.

Although this was the sixth Genesis studio album, it was the first to break even financially, and at time of release, it sold as many copies as all the previous releases combined. Although the earlier albums earned gold and platinum awards, it often took ten years or more to accumulate the required sales, frequently driven by legions of new fans exploring the back catalogue. Of the bands new found success, Gabriel claimed his ego was 'twinged', saying:

I was happy that the people I'd known from childhood did well, but when I fronted the band, everyone assumed I did everything, and now I had left, and they were more successful, people assumed I had done nothing.

This was also the first album where individual band members – or smaller groups – received their own writing credits. Banks felt it was unfair that with an imbalance in the writing, every musician should share the credits evenly. He had written a lot of the previous album and had suggested at that time to credit each song to the individual writers, but it wasn't agreed by the rest of the band at the time. Another aim of the new album was to move to a simpler structure for the music, especially after the complexity of *The Lamb Lies Down On Broadway* and 'simplify everything' according to Banks. The result was a very strong statement of intent, and this was a band that were moving on with a fresher sound. Their music was heavier and more bombastic, but with enough references to their past musical highlights to keep fans happy and bring them along on this new journey. David Hentschel was brought in to help the band with the production of the album. He had previously worked with them when he was an engineer at Trident Studios when *Nursery Cryme* was recorded and he would continue to work with the band on the next four studio albums up to and including *Duke*.

For the tour that followed, Bill Bruford – formerly of King Crimson and Yes – was drafted into the band to play drums. Collins was already friends with him but hadn't considered that he would be interested in touring with the band. Bruford was touring with Brand X, having replaced Collins, and commented to him one day 'How come you haven't asked me?' to which Collins replied, 'I didn't think you fancied it'. They met, played a few parts together and the decision was made to bring him in for the tour. The whole atmosphere of a Genesis show changed in 1976 as not only was there a new frontman and two drummers, but other changes were made to fill the obvious void created without Gabriel's stage theatrics. A much larger light show accompanied the tour, and Hackett and Rutherford would stand up for the majority of the concerts (previously they had played sitting down), and both musicians would also take on some of the between-song chat and announcements.

Colin Elgie designed the cover at Hipgnosis. He had no music to listen to, but he was provided with lyrics and was asked to illustrate the characters from the songs. He says he knew the band liked his work because they had him design stationery based on the images he created using the Victorian engraving style, at it seemed to fit the characters in the songs. He also created a new hand-drawn Genesis logo which was used on both *A Trick of the Tail* and *Wind & Wuthering*.

'Dance on a Volcano' 5:55 (Rutherford, Banks, Hackett, Collins)

Much has been written around the meaning of this song, some claiming that its lyrics are a metaphor for the trenches in World War One, mainly due to the mention of green and blue crosses which were used to identify gas shells. I always heard the song in terms of a high-speed adventure; a race to get to the top of an erupting volcano. Lyrics such as 'Dirty old mountain all covered in smoke', and 'Through a crack in Mother Earth, blazing hot, the molten rock, Spills out over the land', suggest a race between man and nature. The alliteration of the line 'And the lava's the lover that licks your boots away' suggest that the mountain is playing a sensual and seductive game with the adventurer. The imagery is of the fight to conquer something which is not easy and presents many obstacles, much like the situation that Genesis found themselves in at the time of writing the album. The race to find a singer and write material before the press discovered the departure of Gabriel must have felt like running up that volcano at times.

One of the first songs to be written in the studio before Hackett re-joined after he completed Voyage Of The Acolyte, it opens with a short, lone Rutherford 'picked' guitar theme, quickly joined by Hackett and Collins playing a series of big, unison fills. Bass pedals and strings further add to the bombastic nature of the introduction. At 4:18, after 'Let the dance begin' we are treated to a high-speed instrumental end with galloping drums and guitar. The pace briefly slows almost to a stop followed by another racing rhythm then slowing to tease the riders at the top of a rise, only to race ahead again, before finally coming to a slow, quiet end.

'Entangled' 6:26 (Hackett, Banks)

A perfect way to come down from the energy and pace of 'Dance on a Volcano', 'Entangled' is a beautiful, predominantly guitar-based piece with mellotron and haunting keyboard solo to finish. The end of the track uses layers of guitars, similar to earlier pieces like 'Stagnation' but with the enhanced production techniques to really make it work. The Banks solo conjures up a dreamy image as if the Lady of the Lake is about to appear. The origins of the song were from Hackett, who had a verse idea in 3/4 while Banks had a chorus in 3/4 'without a home', so they matched them up. 'Entangled' was released as a single in February 1976 with 'A Trick of the Tail' as the B-side, but did not chart.

'Squonk' 6:29 (Rutherford, Banks)

'Squonk' feels like it should have been the first song on the album. While 'Dancing on a Volcano' is still a great, upbeat starter, this is much more direct with a solid beat throughout but no doubt the band wanted to start with a multi-section piece to let their fans know that they were still producing complex arrangements. Collins calls this their attempt at a Led Zeppelin 'Kashmir' or 'When The Levee Breaks' – using a heavier guitar and drum sound compared with their earlier releases. It would be used to open the live set on the *Wind & Wuthering* tour in 1977 and also features on *Seconds Out*.

The Squonk appears in written accounts around the beginning of the 20th Century as a Tasmanian Devil- type creature that lived in the Hemlock forests of Northern Pennsylvania. The stories tell of a creature with an ill-fitting skin, covered in warts. It was so ashamed of its appearance that it would hide, spending most of its time weeping and if captured, it would dissolve completely into a pool of bubbles and tears.

'Mad Man Moon' 7:35 (Banks)

This is a great example of a romantic, Banks-penned ballad with a wonderful lyric about chasing something you don't have, while not appreciating what you do have. This was one of the songs that Banks had expected Collins to sing, even if they had found a new singer. It offers so much more than 'Ripples', the other ballad on the album being more of a 'grower' without the instant likeability of some of the other songs, though the chorus gets an instant thumbs up. The music floats along through two verses before rising to the chorus. What the reference to 'Mad Man Moon' is, remains obscure, perhaps it is another way of 'wishing on a star'. Banks plays some of his best piano on this song, especially in the middle section with synthesiser arpeggios placed on top of piano chords to create an orchestral arrangement reminiscent of Banks' solo work, before returning to the fast-paced 'Sandman' section and closing with another wistful verse. The song was never played live, most likely due to the complexity of the keyboard arrangement in the middle section of the song.

'Robbery, Assault and Battery' 6:16 (Banks, Collins)

This track is where 'The Battle Of Epping Forest' meets 'Cinema Show' in the first of several songs where Collins uses his 'cheeky Cockney', 'Artful Dodger' style characterisation. The lyrics aren't to be taken too seriously, telling of a failed burglar who gets caught but still plans to go back and try again when he gets out. The piece would have made a great instrumental track, and I wasn't convinced by the vocal and lyrics when the album came out. Stylistically, it also suggests 'Get 'em Out By Friday' and 'Harold The Barrel' but without the lyrical bloat of those two pieces. The strong middle section of this is magnificent, portraying a 'cops and robbers' chase sequence, with Banks playing a synth solo that harks back to the earlier days of songs like 'Cinema Show'. It also has some of Collins' best drumming on the album, and after another verse, we have a second great solo from Banks. The song came into its own as a live piece in which Collins would don a hat, scarf and overcoat and act out the story.

'Ripples' 8:06 (Rutherford, Banks)

It may be a little predictable in the track sequencing, but yet again we have a ballad after an upbeat number, here bringing with it the first sign of a commercial side of Genesis via a very catchy chorus. A song about the fading of youth and beauty, it is depicted on the cover as an old woman looking into the mirror and seeing her younger self looking back. 'The face that launched a thousand ships is fading fast, that happens you know', pointing out that even the beauty of Helen of Troy would fade in time, and 'Ripples' being the memory of youth that once gone won't come back.

A typical dreamy twelve string motif from Rutherford carries the verses through to the fuller chorus, the style of which became a Banks signature. The entry to the middle instrumental section at 4:05 feels clumsy, almost a forced change of pace to tag on another idea, but it provides us with a wonderful, swelling solo from Hackett. In comparison, the return from this middle section to the reprise of the chorus is superbly carried off as it builds and merges into the familiar chords of the chorus. The drums, which appear in the second half, have the top end repressed and are pushed to the back of the mix which is a nice touch, in keeping with the mood of the number. The song was released as a single in March 1976 with 'It's Yourself' as the B-side.

'A Trick of the Tail' 4:35 (Banks)

This is another of Banks' songs, based on the book 'The Inheritors' by William Golding. It tells of a race of beings who were on earth before man and in particular, is the story of the last survivor of this race who has horns and a tail and how the inhabitants of a modern city react to him. This was the first Genesis song to have an accompanying video, a simple affair with the band sitting around a piano. However, it is notable for its director, Bruce Gowers, who had previously directed the video for 'Bohemian Rhapsody' by Queen. Gowers also directed videos for 'Ripples' and 'Robbery, Assault and Battery'.

The break doubles the beat at 'And broke down the door of the cage...', and for the first time in a Genesis song, it uses 'doo wops' in the backing vocals. Released as the B-side to 'Entangled' in February 1976, the song was then released as an A-side in March 1976 with 'Ripples' as the B-side, although both failed to chart.

'Los Endos' 5:46 (Collins, Hackett, Rutherford, Banks)

'Los Endos' is a great way to end the album and an ideal way to end the band's set at concerts for many years to come. It came from an idea by Hackett, adapted rhythmically by Collins to form this signature majestic instrumental, complete with a massive sound and a reprise of 'Squonk' at the end. The drumming on this is superb, as the track ebbs and flows through changes of pace and dramatic stops and starts. As the piece closes, Collins sings 'There's an angel standing in the sun, trying to get back home' from 'Supper's Ready', as a nod to the departed Gabriel.

Related tracks
'It's Yourself' 5:26 (Banks, Collins, Hackett, Rutherford)
The main vocal part of this song is quite forgettable, but the middle section was used pretty much intact as the beginning of 'Los Endos'. The song was released twice as a B-side, first on 'Ripples' in March 1976 and later for 'Your Own Special Way' in February 1977 from *Wind & Wuthering*.

Wind & Wuthering (1976)

Personnel:
Phil Collins: voices, drums, cymbals, percussion
Steve Hackett: electric guitars, nylon classical guitar, 12 string guitar, kalimba, autoharp
Mike Rutherford: four,six, and eight string bass guitars, electric and 12 string acoustic guitars, bass pedals
Tony Banks: Steinway grand piano, ARP 2600 synthesiser, ARP Pro Soloist synthesiser, Hammond organ, Mellotron, Roland string synthesiser, Fender Rhodes piano etc
Recorded at Relight Studios, Hilvarenbeek, Netherlands and Trident Studios, London between September and October 1976
Producer: David Hentschel and Genesis
Sleeve design: Hipgnosis
Released: December 17, 1976
Label: Charisma, Atco
Highest Chart places: UK: 7, US: 26. Achieved gold in France (50,000), UK (100,000) and US (500,000).
Running time: 50:54

Wind & Wuthering was something of a surprise, being the second album of 1976 in the UK, and still within twelve months of *A Trick of the Tail* when it was released in January 1977 in the US. Having broken even financially for the first time with *A Trick of the Tail*, followed by a successful tour to promote the release, the band immediately entered the studio to produce a follow up that would capitalise on this success. It would also be the first recording made in a studio outside the UK. Now that there was money to be made, the band were advised to record abroad, as they could retain 25% more of the returns. The band travelled to Relight Studios in Hilvarenbeek, Netherlands, which sounds like a lovely canal escape surrounded by windmills. However, David Hentschel paints a slightly different picture:

> *It was next to a pig farm so it was a fairly rural and fragrant environment in which to have your breakfast! We were all living together for two weeks. It was just us and the road crew. We'd eat at the studio every night, have stuff sent in. It was totally cut off but that enabled us to concentrate. By the time we went into the studio, there was very little to do. Pretty much all of them [the songs] worked straight away, third or fourth take and it was done.*

It is typical of Genesis to be uncompromising, buck any trend and do what they wanted. They would release an album that was both romantic and even progressively 'heavy' as Banks called it, in the same month as the Sex Pistols infamous appearance on Bill Grundy's *Today* show, launching their short eighteen-month career, and punk rock in general, on an unsuspecting British public.

The album is more complex and romantic in some ways than *A Trick of the Tail*, opening with two very strong songs and finishing on a high with a song that was to become a live favourite for many years to come in 'Afterglow'. I disagree with some of the retrospective conjecture that this was the last 'prog' album from Genesis, a view shared by both Hackett and David Hentschel. While the 'proggier' elements would become rarer, there was certainly more complex music to come, especially with *Duke* and also examples on later albums such as 'Fading Lights' from *We Can't Dance*.

It should come as no surprise that the title is inspired by *Wuthering Heights*, the only novel written by Emily Bronte, which suits the romantic thread running through pretty much every song. 'Wuthering' means 'blowing strongly with a roaring sound', a good description of the upbeat nature of the band's mood after the success of *A Trick of the Tail*. The album title was the original name for the two instrumental tracks that became 'Unquiet slumbers for the sleepers... 'and '...in that quiet earth', whose names are taken from the last line of Emily Bronte's great novel.

I lingered round them, under that benign sky: watched the moths fluttering among the heath and harebells, listened to the soft wind breathing through the grass, and wondered how anyone could ever imagine unquiet slumbers for the sleepers in that quiet earth.

Banks calls this their most romantic, and musically ambitious release, containing many of his favourite songs, thus becoming one of his two favourite Genesis albums.

A world tour was planned after the release, lasting over six months. This was to be a major production with a specially designed stage, custom lighting and their own patented laser system, while Chester Thompson from Earth Wind and Fire would join them on drums, replacing Bill Bruford. The first venue would be the re-opening of the world-famous Rainbow Theatre in London on New Year's Day 1977, with three sold out shows, receiving 60,000 applications for the 6,000 tickets. The Paris dates of this tour provided the recordings for the superb live album *Seconds Out*.

Collins and Hackett both had a greater writing role with *Wind & Wuthering* than previously, but it was during this time that Hackett became ever more frustrated with the band's lack of acceptance of his music. He found it increasingly difficult to have ideas accepted and worked on, 'Blood On The Rooftops' being the only song credited to him (except the tracks developed by the whole band and the instrumental track he worked on with Rutherford). From Hackett's perspective, he felt he wasn't being used to his full potential and that his song ideas were being ignored. Collins says he had to fight to get 'Wot Gorilla' accepted, and this was at the expense of 'Please Don't Touch' from Hackett, which would end up on his second solo release (of the same name) in April 1978.

The cover was the second to be designed by Colin Elgie at Hipgnosis. This time all he was given was the title of the album, but he felt it had a great visual quality, conjuring up immediate images of Heathcliff and the moors. He had also seen a movie on TV called The War Lord starring Charlton Heston which included a scene where Heston is next to a tree, and the birds in it fly off, that scene providing the inspiration for the cover. He then painted a watercolour from memory over two or three weeks. In retrospect, he wished he had made a better job of it and added more colour. Elgie also hand drew a combined Genesis and *Wind & Wuthering* logo for the cover using the same Genesis font he had created for *A Trick of the Tail*.

'Eleventh Earl of Mar' 7:39 (Banks, Hackett, Rutherford)

The Eleventh Earl of Mar (or sixth, depending upon which counting method you use) was John Erskine who lived in Alloa near Stirling. Erskine was twice Secretary of State for Scotland under Queen Anne, and due to his tendency to change allegiance from one side to another as it suited his needs, he was also known as Bobbing John. There is a Wetherspoons bar in the town named after him, but today only a tower from the original ancestral home of the Earls of Mar still exists, although it is the largest keep of its kind still standing. Rutherford wrote the lyrics after reading a 'history book about a failed Scottish rising around 1715'. This was an uprising led by John Erskine in support of James Francis Edward Stuart, the 'Old Pretender', not to be confused with his son, Charles Stuart, 'Bonnie' Prince Charlie, the 'Young Pretender' who was part of the later failed uprising in 1745. The Jacobite army made good progress taking many cities, but for some reason after defeating Argyle's army at Sheriffmuir near Stirling, outnumbering them four to one, he failed to advance on Stirling and capitalise on the victory and retreated to Perth. By the time the Pretender arrived in Scotland, the uprising was close to being over. The first line of the song 'The sun had been up for a couple of hours, covered the ground with a layer of gold' comes from the opening line of *The Flight of the Heron* by D. K. Broster, the first book in a trilogy about the later 1745 rebellion, as opposed to this 1715 one. The song is told from the point of view of a young boy who is being told the story by his father as a bedtime story.

Banks had written an opening sequence of what he called 'strange chords', while Hackett wrote the chorus and its chords, with Rutherford adding the words. My favourite lyric describes James Stuart, saying that he 'Couldn't even lift a sword. Dressed too fine and smelling of wine'. Right from the start with the strains of the distant guitar, this is one of the best openers on any Genesis album, with all four musicians contributing some of their best performances to date. Hackett plays some superb guitar, Rutherford provides a driving baseline, Collins is solid as usual with as many fills as he can fit in without overdoing it if that is possible, and Banks binds it together with organ and synthesiser, keeping his solos short and sympathetic to the material. Slowing only once around the four-minute mark for a short acoustic guitar section and the lullaby 'Time to go to bed now, never seems too keen' bringing us back to the boy who is having this story read to him. The track endings with another rousing verse and a reprise of the opening keyboard and guitar section.

'One for the Vine' 9:59 (Banks)

Banks had written this song over several months in 1976, originally for *A Trick of the Tail*, but he kept working on it until completing the piece later in the year. The lyrics were influenced by Michael Moorcock's fantasy novel *Phoenix in Obsidian,* the second book in the *Eternal Champion* series.

After the energy of 'The Eleventh Earl Of Mar,' the lovely opening section of this song bring us back down to earth. Another song about taking men into a hopeless battle '50 thousand men were sent to do the will of one,' Banks wrote this from multiple ideas and says he loved being able to splice sections of music together and bring in key changes and chords that wouldn't be expected in a pop song. Not that this could ever be considered a 'pop song', featuring as it does multiple layers of keyboards and synthesiser solos. In fact, the only guitar in evidence is in the first few seconds, reprised later, and the closing section. The middle section of the piece is almost all Banks with a sprinkle of percussion and bass. Strong recurrent themes fill the ten minutes here without it feeling too long.

'Your Own Special Way' 6:15 (Rutherford)

This song was the only single to be released from the album in February 1977, with 'It's Yourself' as the B-side. It reached number 43 in the UK charts and provided minor chart success in the US, albeit at number 62 with Rutherford saying that it gave them 'the start of a tickle in America.' It would be another ten years until the *Invisible Touch* album and the major chart success that came with it. It is another song where Rutherford used a long since forgotten 12 string tuning, and while the verse is simple enough, sung in falsetto, it is the chorus that is the star here. Commercial, catchy and with layers of harmonies from Collins, it is a hint of what was to come in later years. A quiet instrumental section combining guitar and keyboards can be found on the album version but was removed for the single.

'Wot Gorilla?' 3:12 (Collins, Banks)

Collins had been recording and playing live with Brand X and was also a big fan of Weather Report and it shows in this track. It is a piece of Jazz fusion that would not have been out of place on a Brand X album. However, it doesn't really go anywhere with a simple keyboard refrain on top that hints that this was a drum rhythm from Collins to which Banks added a solo. Perhaps it would have worked better as part of a longer song. It is the albums weakest track, edging out Hackett's rather better 'Please Don't Touch', about which the guitarist was understandably a bit bitter. In interviews in 1984 and 2007 he called it.

A very inferior instrumental, a real doodle of an idea. 'Wot Gorilla' was good rhythmically but underdeveloped harmonically. Dispassionately, I think 'Please Don't Touch' has both rhythm and harmonic development, which is more exciting.

It was one of the incidents that would eventually see him leave the group after the subsequent tour.

'All in a Mouse's Night' 6:35 (Banks)

Based on the cartoon series *Tom and Jerry*, this is a whimsical tale from Banks. He feels it is the poorest of his three tracks, saying

I don't feel it's my most successful track. The riffs were good, but the lyric was a little self-conscious. I don't think it's bad; it's just not up there with my other two.

There are some memorable parts to this piece and the galloping, tongue-twisting section the starts with 'The door's been opened, my chance to escape. Must run out quick, better sorry than late.' mirrors the chase and panic of the mouse. For me, the best part is the instrumental section at the end which has a great Hackett solo over a strong keyboard accompaniment, complete with a church organ.

'Blood on the Rooftops' 5:20 (Hackett, Collins)

Hackett was finding it hard to get his ideas accepted by the band, and even harder to have them recorded especially after the flexibility he had enjoyed while recording *Voyage of the Acolyte*. This was the sixth studio release by Genesis that Hackett worked on, and by now he was beginning to feel that it should have 25% of his music accepted. It is a dark song about couch potatoes that watch the world go by on the TV. Hackett wrote the verse and the lyrics, while Collins came up with the melody for the chorus and the title. The lyrics provide an interesting social commentary of the time via many references to UK television. In 1976 the UK only had three TV channels to choose from and one of those, BBC2, only transmitted in the evening. *Batman, Tarzan* and *The Streets Of San Francisco* were three shows imported from the US, while *The Wednesday Play* was a series of one-off dramas that had ended in 1970 to be replaced by *Play For Today*, which didn't fit so well lyrically, one suspects. 'The Queen on Christmas Day' refers to that wonderfully British tradition of watching the Queen's speech, broadcast at 3 pm on Christmas day every year.

Banks says this has always been one of his favourite Genesis tracks. It certainly stands out, particularly because the use of the classical nylon string

Left: During the 'She's a lady' section at the end of 'The Musical Box', Gabriel would stumble back onto the stage wearing a grotesque mask, portraying the old man of the story. The photos on this page are from the Shepperton Studios live show in 1973.

Right: This flower mask was one of many used by Gabriel during performances of 'Supper Ready', worn during the 'Willow Farm' section, illustrating the lyric 'Narcissus is turned to a flower'.

Left: Gabriel wore this iconic Britannia costume during the introduction and early sections of 'Dancing With the Moonlit Knight' from *Selling England By The Pound*. The costume symbolised the UK of the past, swept aside in the wave of commercialisation and perceived loss of identity that was the theme of the album, released in 1973.

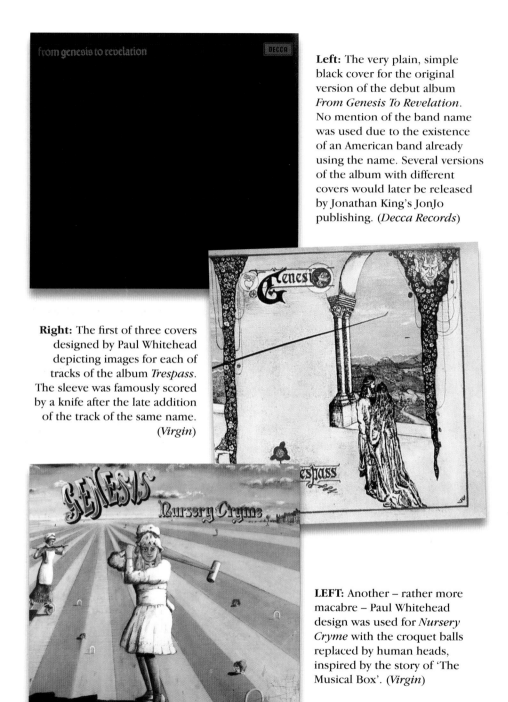

Left: The very plain, simple black cover for the original version of the debut album *From Genesis To Revelation*. No mention of the band name was used due to the existence of an American band already using the name. Several versions of the album with different covers would later be released by Jonathan King's JonJo publishing. (*Decca Records*)

Right: The first of three covers designed by Paul Whitehead depicting images for each of tracks of the album *Trespass*. The sleeve was famously scored by a knife after the late addition of the track of the same name. (*Virgin*)

LEFT: Another – rather more macabre – Paul Whitehead design was used for *Nursery Cryme* with the croquet balls replaced by human heads, inspired by the story of 'The Musical Box'. (*Virgin*)

Right: An original vinyl copy of *Foxtrot*, released in October 1972. This was the last of the three Paul Whitehead covers. The cover painting inspired Gabriel to appear on stage in Dublin wearing his wife's red dress and a fox's head. (*Virgin, from the author's collection*)

Left: A modified painting by Royal Academy artist Betty Swanwick was used for *Selling England By The Pound*. Rarely for the group, they all agreed that this was a great cover. (*Virgin*)

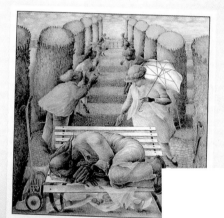

Right: The double concept album *The Lamb Lies Down On Broadway* took a different design approach with the first of the covers from Hipgnosis. The main character, Rael, is depicted in several scenes from the story by an actor credited as Omar on the sleeve notes. (*Virgin*)

Above: The classic five-piece Genesis line up in 1973, with Gabriel on flute, again taken from the live film shot at Shepperton Studios in 1973, as are all the pictures on the next two pages.

Left: Steve Hackett in his typical seated playing position. It would be the 1976 *A Trick of the Tail* tour before he would perform standing up.

Right: Tony Banks concentrates while playing the Hohner Pianet N which sat on top of his Mellotron M400. At this point in the band's history, he was also using a Hammond T-102 organ with an ARP Pro Soloist synthesiser on top, in his live rig.

Left: Phil Collins when he played a rather smaller drum kit than in later tours. Note the inventive rigging for assorted percussion behind him, made from Dexion shelving uprights.

Right: Rutherford is renowned for playing a double-neck Rickenbacker or Shergold guitar, allowing him to move quickly between bass guitar and six-string rhythm guitar parts. While playing rhythm, he would often use bass pedals to replace the bass guitar.

Left: Rutherford and Hackett both playing 12-string acoustic guitars at the start of 'Suppers Ready'. Banks would also play the intro part on 12-string before moving to the piano.

Above: The original *A Trick of the Tail* album cover, released in February 1976, with Colin Elgie's Victorian-style engravings inspired by characters from each of the eight songs. (*Virgin*)

Above: For the second album of 1976, the *Wind & Wuthering* cover used a haunting, misty watercolour landscape with a solitary tree. (*Virgin*)

Left: A portrait of John Erskine, the Eleventh Earl of Mar, that hangs in a family tower in Alloa, Scotland. The story of his 1715 Jacobite uprising inspired Rutherford to write the opening song for *Wind & Wuthering*. (*Stuart Macfarlane*)

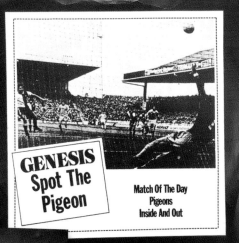

Right: The *Spot The Pigeon* EP cover from 1977, with three additional tracks recorded during the *Wind & Wuthering* sessions. (*Virgin, from the author's collection*)

Left: The cover for the 1978 release … *and then there were three*… was another from Hipgnosis, showing three shady characters at night. The light trails represent the comings and goings within the band. (*Virgin*)

Right: The *Duke* Cover in 1980 was the last of a long line of Hipgnosis designs based on illustrations by Lionel Koechlin, depicting Albert gazing out of the window at the moon. The album was recorded at ABBA's studio in Stockholm. (*Virgin*)

Dear all,
Just a brief note to let you all know what we'll be doing in '79. After having had a well-earned rest in January and February following our back-breaking tours last year, we will start work on a new studio album around March on which both Daryl and Chester will probably be featured. This should be ready for release around June or July. As for touring, we have an English tour lined up in October in which we hope to be playing some of the smaller theatres. We have also, all recently acquired relatively sophisticated recording equipment in our homes, and so hopefully there may be a few solo projects on the way as well.

On a personal level the original 'Samox' may be reforming again to make another album and all of us will be joining forces with both Rod Argent and Alphonso Johnson to play a few selected dates around London during February.

Well, that just about covers it .... Happy New Year from all of us ...

Phil Collins
PHIL COLLINS

Above: A copy of a handwritten letter from Phil Collins which was sent out to Genesis fan club members at the start of 1977 describing the plans the band had for the new year. (*Stuart Macfarlane*)

Left: A fan club newsletter from January 1979 after the band returned from their first tour of Japan. This was one of the few ways to keep in touch with what the band were doing in a pre-Internet age. (*Stuart Macfarlane*)

Right: The sleeve for the *3x3* 7-inch vinyl EP release. The three band members are shown jumping in the air, in a pastiche of The Beatles *Twist And Shout* EP. (*Virgin, from the author's collection*)

Left: The cover for the 1981 album *Abacab*. This abstract design came in four colour schemes and was chosen to highlight the more abstract nature of the content which signified another change in musical direction. (*Virgin*)

Right: The *Genesis* cover from 1983 featuring plastic pieces from the children's Tupperware toy Shape-O which led to it being referred to by many as the 'shapes' album. (*Virgin*)

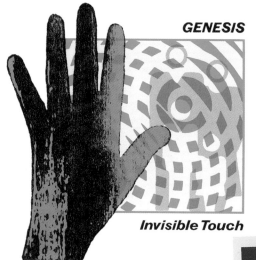

GENESIS

Invisible Touch

Left: The most commercially successful album from Genesis, *Invisible Touch* was released in 1986. The cover was a confusing affair showing an abstract depiction of a family of four surrounded by a grid with the large hand reaching out towards them. The idea behind it is somewhat obscure, and it's dated rather badly. (*Virgin*)

Right: A flyer with travel offers to see the band at Madison Square Gardens, New York, where they played five nights in 1986. It was sent to Genesis fan club members. (*Stuart Macfarlane*)

GENESIS
MADISON SQUARE GARDEN, NEW YORK

New York, New York. The world's most exciting city — Manhattan, Broadway, Central Park, all night nightlife in the city that never sleeps... and see GENESIS live in concert at MADISON SQUARE GARDEN!

Our long weekend to New York will be a non-stop party with four fabulous nights in a centrally located hotel, flights with Virgin Atlantic from Gatwick to Newark and of course your tickets to see GENESIS will be included in the price.

We'll be flying you to America on Wednesday, far October arriving in New York early enough for you to check in to your hotel and still have plenty of time and energy to enjoy your first night in the Big Apple. Your tickets to see Genesis will be for either the Thursday or Friday night — on the other nights of your stay you might like to see a show, visit a club or disco — full details of all the options we can arrange for you will be included on your travel information.

Accommodation will be at either the Milford Plaza or the Century Paramount Hotel, both very comfortable, centrally located hotels within easy reach of a multitude of restaurants and entertainment centres. All rooms have private bathroom/wc., air conditioning, television and radio.

The homeward flight will be late on Sunday so even on your last day you'll still be able to do a whole lot more than just the packing!

The price for this fabulous package is just £449 which includes:
• Ticket to see GENESIS live at Madison Square Garden
• Return flight with Virgin Atlantic from London to Newark
• All in flight meals and entertainment
• Four nights' accommodation in central New York
• Transfers from the airport to your hotel on arrival and back to the airport when you depart
• The services of an MGP representative during your stay
• Insurance against concert cancellation
• All airport taxes and service charges

It does not include:
• Local transportation (other than stated above)
• Meals during your stay
• Personal insurance which will cost £25.00 and must be paid with your deposit

To reserve your place(s) on this tour just complete the booking form overleaf and rush it back to MGP (International Concert Travel).

VIRGIN

land of confusion

gene

Left: The single sleeve from 'Land Of Confusion'. The three *Spitting Image* puppet heads used in the video are arranged in the style of The Beatles album *With The Beatles*. (*Virgin, from the author's collection*)

Right: For the last studio album with Collins in 1991, the *We Can't Dance* cover uses a playful painting from Felicity Roma Bowers depicting a father and son gazing skywards on a hill, or just possibly a very tiny planet. Yet another new Genesis logo was designed to accompany this release. (*Virgin*)

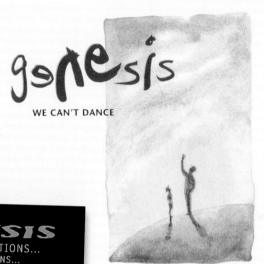

Left: The rather uninspired sleeve design for the last studio album released by Genesis, *Calling All Stations* in 1997. (*Virgin*).

Right: A rather young-looking Ray Wilson at a show in 1998. He was 30 at the time of the live shows for *Calling All Stations*. He is still performing songs from all eras of Genesis as part of his live performances and sang 'Carpet Crawlers' with Steve Hackett in Glasgow in 2013.

Left: The cover of *Genesis Live*, released in 1973. The image used shows Gabriel in his 'Magog' mask that was worn during 'Suppers Ready', even though the track did not appear on the original version of the album. (*Virgin*)

Above: Live shots of the band from the inside of an original vinyl copy of *Seconds Out*, released in October 1977. The sleeve also used photos from the 1976 tour with Bill Bruford on drums, though only 'Cinema Show' was used from that tour. (*Virgin, from the author's collection*)

Right: The front of the *Seconds Out* cover featured the double row of incredibly bright 747 aircraft landing lights used to great effect on the *Wind & Wuthering* tour of 1977. (*Virgin*)

Right: In contrast to the often visually stunning artwork used by the band, another simplistic and rather dull design was chosen for the *Three Sides Live* Cover in 1982. (*Virgin*)

Below: The *Live Over Europe* cover uses a design drawing for the huge and spectacular stage, screen and lighting setup for the 2007 tour. The design from Stufish Entertainment Architects featured a 250-foot-wide custom curved LED screen that took three hours to erect at every concert. (*Virgin*)

Above: Originally released as separate CDs in 1993, the two volumes of *The Way We Walk*, The Shorts and The Longs were combined into a double CD for the 2009 box set *Genesis Live 1973-2007*. The tracks were re-ordered to closely match the original 1992 tour setlist, while the cover for the combined version used the image from *The Shorts* CD. (*Virgin*)

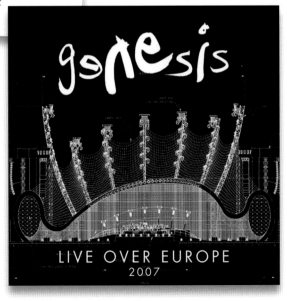

Above: Banks looks amused as he is introduced to the audience by Collins before playing 'No Son Of Mine' in Dusseldorf in 2007. The concert was broadcast live to cinemas around Europe, and the pictures on the next two pages are taken from that concert.

Below: Collins during the 'Ha Ha' section of 'Mama' trying – and probably succeeding – to scare any young children in the audience. For most of the song, the stage was bathed in blue light with the band dramatically lit in red.

Above: A side view of the stage showing how small the area for the band was compared with the overall size of the construction, dominated by the LED display and lighting rigs.

Below: Rutherford plays rhythm guitar during 'Land Of Confusion' in 2007. He would trade rhythm, lead and bass guitar duties with Daryl Stuermer throughout the set.

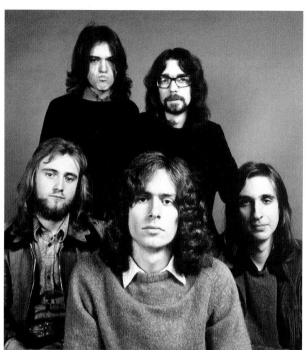

Left: A publicity shot of the classic five-piece band, taken around 1971. (*Virgin*)

Below: The three-piece 'pop' era Genesis during the launch event for the 2007 reunion tour, with Collins ever the joker. (*Virgin*)

guitar by Hackett, contrasting with the much used 12-string arrangements favoured by the band. It follows the pattern of many Hackett songs that were to come, with its quiet verse and big, upbeat chorus.

'Unquiet slumbers for the sleepers...' 2:27 (Hackett, Rutherford)

Coupled with the following track, as mentioned, the titles of these two instrumentals reference the last line of *Wuthering Heights* by Emily Bronte. This part is slow and emotive, cinematic in parts with multiple guitar textures and a haunting, whistling synth melody line from Banks. There is no apparent need to have the tracks split as they run together anyway, but Banks had always wanted to use an ellipsis in a song title, so this was the perfect excuse to use it. Twice.

'...in that quiet earth' 4:45 (Hackett, Rutherford, Banks, Collins)

Following on directly from the previous track but in a much heavier vein, this piece provides the perfect build-up to 'Afterglow'. It is the only track on the album that is credited to the whole band, and it certainly sounds like it was developed in a studio jam session. The piece is about as heavy as Genesis get, both driving and rocking, with reverse guitars, and multiple sections and solos it blasts along, building and changing much like 'Apocalypse in 9/8' from 'Supper's Ready'. The second half transforms once again to a heavier stomp in the vein of Led Zeppelin 'Kashmir' with wilder solos until it slows to a single chord that will take us into ...

'Afterglow' 4:10 (Banks)

'Afterglow' is a powerful love ballad from the point of view of a person who has lost someone very dear to them, 'For now, I have lost everything. I give to you, my soul'. Banks has said that this was about the last person on earth in the afterglow of the apocalypse, having lost everyone they knew and loved, offering their soul and welcoming their own end.

The song was written in 'about as long as it took to play' according to Banks, but after a few days, he realised the first few lines of the verse sounded like 'Have Yourself a Merry Little Christmas.' He has since convinced himself that it doesn't, but check it out for yourself, I still think it does. This song became a favourite on tours for over ten years either with '... in that quiet earth' initially preceding it, then the 'Old Medley' on later tours. On Seconds Out only 'Afterglow' is used from the live recordings and it loses much of its impact without the instrumental build-up. Coupled with the elaborate light shows with which the band toured, this was a high point in any show. Much of the song, particularly the end section, features a choir of multi-tracked vocal 'Ahhs' from Collins, which was inspired by the 10cc track 'I'm Not In Love'.

Related tracks

At least three additional tracks were recorded in the same sessions, 'Match Of The Day', 'Pigeons' and 'Inside and Out' and were released on the *Spot The Pigeon* EP.

Spot the Pigeon EP (1977)

Personnel:
Tony Banks: keyboards
Phil Collins: drums, percussion, vocals
Steve Hackett: guitars
Mike Rutherford: guitars, bass guitar
Recorded at Relight Studios, Hilvarenbeek, the Netherlands between September and October 1976
Producer: David Hentschel and Genesis
Sleeve design: Hipgnosis
Released: 20 May 1977
Label: Charisma
Highest Chart places: UK: 14, US: Not released. Achieved silver in the UK (60,000) and gold in Germany (100,000)
Running time: 13:21

Three previously unreleased songs that were originally recorded during the sessions for *Wind & Wuthering* were released on a 7-inch EP (Extended Play) single in Europe. It gave the band their first UK chart hit since 'I Know What I Like' peaking at number 14. This was the first of two EPs that did not see a release in the US as the format was not a popular one. The tracks would later form part of *Archive 2: 1976 – 1992* released in 2000, and again in 2007 on the *Turn It On Again: The Hits, The Tour Edition*.

The sleeve was again designed by Hipgnosis and is a play on the 'spot the ball' newspaper competition, where the ball would be edited out from a photograph of a football match. The challenge was to place one cross or more to mark where you thought the ball was.

'Match of the Day' 3:24 (Banks, Collins, Rutherford)

None of the band ever thought the song was very good, with rambling – arguably embarrassing – lyrics about English football. *Match of the Day* was a Saturday night show on BBC television where the best action from that day's football would be shown and debated. It is still with us.

'Pigeons' 3:12 (Banks, Collins, Rutherford)

If you ever wondered who put 50 tons of faeces on the foreign office roof, then wonder no more, as this song has the answer. Banks says it was a lot of fun to write and record, especially the use of a single note to work chords under, which the band had wanted to do for a while. It is, however, the weakest of the songs recorded at the time, bouncing along but never really going anywhere.

'Inside and Out' 6:45 (Banks, Collins, Hackett, Rutherford)

This is the best of the three songs by a long way. It is a story of wrongful imprisonment and subsequent release, which make up the two distinct parts of the song. Banks says that the solos he and Hackett were quite eccentric with the solos in the second 'Out' part, with Hackett playing the solo in a similar style to Steve Howe of Yes. The introduction and verse use a lush twelve-string guitar arrangement, and the piece has a mournful vocal from Collins.

...and then there were three... (1978)

Personnel:
Tony Banks: keyboards
Phil Collins: drums, percussion, vocals
Mike Rutherford: basses, guitars
Recorded at Relight Studios, Hilvarenbeek, the Netherlands between September and October 1977
Producer: David Hentschel and Genesis
Sleeve design: Hipgnosis
Released: March 28 1978 in the US and March 31 1978 in the UK
Label: Charisma
Highest Chart places: UK: 3, US: 14. Achieved platinum in the US (1,000,000) and gold in France (50,000), UK (100,000) and Germany (100,000).
Running time: 53:27

Journalist Chris Welch, a great supporter of the band, used the headline 'And then there were three' in Melody Maker to announce Hackett's departure, which inspired the band to give the album such a name. Rutherford remembers an interview in which he was asked where the title came from, and he thought, 'oh dear, this is going to be a long one'.

Forced, once again, to consider the future of the band with another member gone, the decision was made to continue as a three-piece with Rutherford taking on all the guitar parts, at least in the studio. The quantity of guitar that Rutherford had already contributed to the band's music is often overlooked, and he regularly played rhythm guitar while Hackett concentrated on lead. On this album, there are sections where the lack of lead guitar is a disappointment and it is somewhat sparse throughout the album. Rutherford would improve his playing over time, but as a lead player, he would never come close to Hackett's skill level and individuality. Rutherford now looks back at this period and considers this the poorest record the band made, though not everyone feels the same, of course.

But For me, the album is inconsistent and the poorest since the departure of Gabriel. While previously the writing contributions of Hackett had often been limited, his ability to add subtle support to the arrangements was very much missed on this album. While a few notable highlights exist in 'Many Too Many', 'Snowbound' and even 'Follow You, Follow Me', much of the material was a learning exercise that would not come to fruition until Duke.

However, both Banks and Rutherford say that being a three-piece made things easier, allowing more space for each of the three writers. That said, the writing on the album was pretty much split between Rutherford and Banks, almost as if they'd made half a solo album each. Despite this, they both went on to record solo albums shortly after – Smallcreep's Day (Rutherford) and A Curious Feeling (Banks) – which reached number 13 and 21 respectively in the UK charts. Banks later claimed that the loss of Gabriel and Hackett was made more bearable, as they were lucky enough have access to another singer and another guitarist in the band. This view trivialises the impact both departed musicians had on the development of the sound of Genesis. Without Gabriel, *The Lamb* would never have been recorded, and without Hackett, his signature guitar style would not have become an integral part of the overall sound of the band.

The theme running through almost every track on the album is that of death and loss, although it isn't necessarily apparent without close attention to the lyrics. Both the cover and the music have the feeling of a dark winter about them. There had been a conscious decision, to attempt to write simpler, shorter songs, with only two tracks, over six minutes long. The cover was another from Hipgnosis, featuring a time lapsed photograph with the light trails intended to represent the comings and goings within the band, according to Storm Thorgerson of Hipgnosis. The Genesis logo used on the cover was a version of the angular logo from *The Lamb*.

The album reached number three in the UK charts and fourteen in the US, achieving a platinum award in that territory. Part of this success was down to a huge tour of over nine months taking in almost 100 shows. Daryl Stuermer was brought in on guitar and bass coupled with Chester Thompson who had already played on the *Wind & Wuthering* tour. Apart from the *Calling All Stations* tour, this quintet was to form the basis of the Genesis live band for the next 30 years, up to including the reunion tour in 2007. The band and their management knew that to make the new line up work, they had to tour America extensively, playing everywhere they could, and they did just that, with three separate America legs of the tour totalling over 50 shows. Collins says that this gruelling tour contributed to the breakup of his first marriage, with his wife Andy moving to Vancouver with their two children to be near her parents. After the tour, Collins told Rutherford and Banks that he was moving to Vancouver to try to save the marriage, and if they couldn't exist as a band living in separate countries, then he was out of Genesis. They were both supportive of his decision and decided to take a break to do solo albums.

'Down and Out' 5:26 (Collins, Banks, Rutherford)

Some high keyboard strings form the introduction to this song, before kicking off the album in a similar vein to *A Trick of the Tail* with an upbeat, bass-driven song about record labels who drop artists who are no longer popular, with the verse from the labels point of view, the chorus from that of the artist. The label says: 'I don't want to beat about the bush, but none of us are getting any younger. There's people out there who could take your place. A more commercial view! A fresher face!' The artist replies, 'Well show me the door, show me someone who'll do it better'.

As the first track we hear from Genesis without Hackett, Rutherford's guitar is prominent in the verse and chorus but mixed very low at the end of the song where there might otherwise have been a bold and rousing solo from Hackett.

Rutherford admits that it took a few albums to gain his confidence as a lead player and in the initial live shows, Stuermer would usually play Hackett's parts as he was a more confident player than Rutherford.

'Undertow' 4:46 (Banks)

The second track has music and lyrics from Banks and is a piano-driven ballad, lifted by some superb lyrics. It raises the question of how to deal with your impending demise, 'If this were the last day of your life, my friend. Tell me what would you think you would do then?'. One reaction might be the philosophical, carpe diem approach of 'Stand up to the blow that fate has struck upon you. Make the most of all you still have coming to you' and another might be despair in 'Lay down on the ground and let the tears run from you. Crying to the grass and trees and heaven finally on your knees'. It is easy to race through life at a pace that barely allows for a pause, and the song tries to remind us that life is precious and finite, and that old age is a privilege, not a guarantee, 'Why do a single thing today. There's tomorrow, sure as I'm here'. So the days they turn into years. And still, no tomorrow appears'.

The song also hints at the plight of homelessness. It is cold outside, it will soon be snowing, there is a northeast wind, the curtains are drawn, and the fire warms the room. A thought crosses the protagonist's mind that there are people outside in this weather, homeless, not tucked up in front of a warm fire, 'And some there are. Cold, they prepare for a sleepless night. Maybe this will be their last fight'. Each night in winter could be your last when you are sleeping rough.

'Ballad of Big' 4:50 (Collins, Banks, Rutherford)

This song tells a cowboy story about lawman Big Jim Cooley, the 'Big' of the title, who gives up his badge in favour of a bet to take a herd over the plain after being called a coward. One night on the trail, while sleeping they are jumped, and all, including Big, died with their boots on. The song was pieced together from an introduction, verse and chorus written by each member of the band, which, in such a relatively short piece, creates some awkward transitions, especially where the galloping rhythm of the opening verses give way to a steadier beat in the 'He got scared' section.

'Snowbound' 4:31 (Rutherford)

'Snowbound' is a beautiful song with rather creepy lyrics. After lying down at midnight and being covered in snow, our protagonist awakes to the delight of children coming to play with the snowman, 'Like a sleeper whose eyes. Sees the pain with surprise. As it smothers your cries'. The horrific thoughts are replaced in the chorus with the optimism of a child in 'Hey there's a Snowman'. The chorus also tells us that 'They say a snow year's a good year. Filled with the love of all who lie so deep'. Winter and the passing of the year is a traditional time for reflection and remembrance of those who have passed on. The song also plays on the fact that Winter is a time that often reminds us of our own mortality, and the struggle of many to get through it and welcome another Spring. A lush arrangement of layered acoustic guitars in the verse serves as a reminder of how much of both acoustic and rhythm guitar Rutherford contributed in the studio, while Banks plays one of his typical haunting piano and synthesiser melody lines through the verse, rising to the ethereal floating chorus packed with strings and flute.

'Burning Rope' 7:09 (Banks)

Lyrically, this follows a similar theme to 'Undertow' with the references to living life to the full, 'Don't live today for tomorrow like you were immortal' and pointing out that the only survivors on our world are the sun, wind and rain. Rutherford's lead guitar is more predominant here than on most of the album, and he pulls off a good solo, though he does try too hard to sound like Hackett at times with the latter's trademark note bending and swelling volume pedal.

'Deep in the Motherlode' 5:15 (Rutherford)

This is a story about the gold rush and how the protagonist is pushed by their family to 'Go West young man', it was used to open the set during the *Duke* tour and its grand introductory chords, and heartbeat verse are reminiscent of older songs such as 'The Cage' or 'Back In New York City'. Banks' use of big, fat chords throughout the song is impressive, giving the song a much heavier feel. This tone marked a welcome change from the band, the remaining three members taking the opportunity to experiment and expand their sound palate as they once again transition to another phase of their career. It is no surprise, then, that the working title was 'Heavy'. The end of the piece disappoints, however, as it fades off into a single chord with reverse drums, guitar and an odd, distant synth solo. It might have been more effective to have ended on a dramatic, modified version of 'Go west young man' motif, as they did when the band played it live.

'Many Too Many' 3:31 (Banks)

This is a slow, delicate ballad about rejection by a protagonist who seems to have been with many others before, 'Many, too many have stood where I stand now', and features Rutherford on lead guitar. One of the early signs of the softer, more commercial side to the band, it didn't sit well with many fans who saw this and 'Follow You, Follow Me' as indicators of a significant change in direction and a departure from their progressive roots. However, I still have a soft spot for this song. I was eighteen when it was released and just starting to discover my 'sensitive side', so it was one of my favourite slow songs at the time. The arrangement is simple but perfect for the track, Banks' piano and Rutherford's lead guitar combining to produce a memorable, haunting backing to Collins' melancholic delivery of the words. Released in the UK on 30 June

1978 as the second single from the album with 'The Day The Lights Went Out' and 'Vancouver' on the B-side, it peaked at number 43. It was not released as a single in the USA.

'Scenes From a Night's Dream' 3:29 (Collins, Banks)

This is a simple story of Little Nemo and his fantastical dreams, based on the comic strip by Winsor McCay which appeared in the *New York Herald*. It is a deceptively short song given the number of words and the storyline it covers, and with music from Banks and lyrics from Collins, it features Rutherford extensively on both rhythm and lead guitars. Saved somewhat by a great bassline and the recurrent opening theme, the song peters out at the end with another reprise of the opening theme, suggesting that the band were running out of options. Always wanting to avoid being accused of repeating himself, Banks had a great affinity with shorter songs, but in this case, it is a shame as it could have developed into an impressive longer piece, making use of the fantasy storytelling element and developing the musical themes further.

'Say It's Alright Joe' 4:20 (Rutherford)

This is a slower song concerning a person in a bar feeling sorry for themselves and asking for reassurance. A simple piano vies with some glorious guitar throughout, breaking into a contrasting chorus for the 'There were Kings who were laughing in the rain' section. However, this is another of the songs which have an unfinished feel, fading out having lost momentum. The live version benefited from Collins' acting out the character in raincoat and cloth cap and also benefitted from a tighter arrangement. The original master tapes of this song were lost, and as a result, there is no remixed version of it on the 2007 release.

'The Lady Lies' 6:07 (Banks)

This is a fairy tale with a twist. After rescuing a fair maiden, our hero is lured into the woods, and we never hear of him again. The chorus of 'Come with me I need you. I fear the dark, and I live all alone. I'll give wine and food too. And something special after if you like', sounds very inviting, but as the title tells us, 'The Lady Lies'. The song provides a vehicle for Banks to open up with a flowing playing style, via an extended synthesiser solo.

'Follow You Follow Me' 3:59 (Rutherford, Banks, Collins)

The album closer is a straightforward, simple pop ballad, and the first top ten hit for the band. Released in the UK on 25 February 1978 with 'Ballad of Big' as the B-side, it reached number seven in the UK charts. It was released a month later in the US with 'Inside and Out' from the *Spot The Pigeon* EP as the B-side and reached number 23 with the success of the single doubling the sales of the album. By the late seventies it was becoming increasingly difficult to maintain a successful career on LP sales alone, so exposure to the singles chart was key, with Banks commenting 'It came at a very key point in our career and was the only reason Genesis were able to exist in an era when singles became more important. We managed without singles up until the late seventies but after that, there were very few groups who could get anywhere without a hit single, and I don't really think Genesis would have been the exception'.

Rutherford wrote the lyrics and recalls it taking about ten minutes to write as it was simple, direct and inspired by his wife, Angie. It was one of the few songs the band had written about love or romance with Banks remarking: 'I was a repressed person' more likely to write based on a great novel or classical Greek mythology. It did help change the audience mix from a mainly male crowd to more females, and this mix would increase with subsequent releases and the development of Collins' solo career, with the song even becoming a popular first dance song at weddings. The song was never originally intended as a single and was slated to end up as a part of a longer piece, but it worked as a short song, something the band had difficulty writing at that point in their career.

The intro is simple with the riff played by Rutherford through an MXR Flanger pedal to produce an airy, sweeping feel. Banks joins him with a simple chord progression and light drum accompaniment. With Hackett gone and Rutherford, whom by his own admission '... wasn't a lead guitarist', lacking confidence, the solo fell to Banks, who plays a floaty run at the end of the song which, like the rest of the track, is simple but works beautifully.

Related tracks
'The Day the Light Went Out' 3:12 (Banks)
Initially suggesting 'Pinball Wizard' by the Who, this up-tempo piece suffers from rather overdone reverb, making the lyrics almost unintelligible. It delivers an apocalyptic story of darkness blocking out the sun, which fails to appear one morning, eventually wiping out much of humanity, not dissimilar to the effects of a nuclear winter. The whole song has an 'old school' Genesis feel to it, with the middle eight – sung in falsetto by Collins – sounding like a throwback to the Gabriel period of the band. With more work and polish this could easily have replaced one of the weaker tracks on the main album. The song was released as one of the B-sides on 'Many Too Many', in June 1978.

'Vancouver' 3:01 (Collins, Rutherford)
This short, easy listening song is about a girl leaving her parents home. There are obvious comparisons to the break up of Collin's marriage and his attempts to rescue it by following his wife to her home town of Vancouver. The song sounds raw and unfinished and is weaker than many of the others included on the album, so is correctly placed as a B-side. In particular, the use of wood blocks through the song's almost entire length is slightly annoying. The song was released as one of the B-sides on 'Many Too Many', in June 1978.

Duke (1980)

Personnel:
Tony Banks: keyboards, backing vocals, 12-string guitar, duck
Mike Rutherford: guitars, basses, backing vocals
Phil Collins: drums, vocals, drum machine, percussion, duck
Recorded at Polar Studios, Stockholm, Sweden between November and December 1979
Producer: David Hentschel and Genesis
Sleeve design: Hipgnosis with illustrations from Lionel Koechlin
Released: March 24 1980, in the US, March 28 1980, in the UK
Label: Charisma
Highest Chart places: UK: 1, US: 11. Achieved platinum in the UK (300,000) and US (1,000,000) and gold in France (50,000).
Running time: 54:59

Duke was the first Genesis album to reach number one in the UK charts, the first of five consecutive number one releases. It heralded the start of a major upswing in the band's popularity, building on the success of ...*and then there were three...* and the single 'Follow You Follow Me'. The album would see them play the last of their theatre tours before moving to larger indoor venues, stadiums and festivals. The release was pivotal in many ways, coming after a two-year break following the long tour promoting ...*and then there were three...* For a fourth time, the future of the band was in question, and there was no guarantee that the band would record together again. Banks later commented that he started work on *A Curious Feeling* so that he would have something to worry about other than Genesis. During the break, Rutherford also released *Smallcreep's Day*. Collins had moved to Vancouver to try to save his marriage, but after a couple of months, realising a divorce was inevitable, he returned to the UK to find Rutherford and Banks busy with their solo albums, so he filled the time touring with Brand X and writing songs for what would become his own solo debut *Face Value*. He says that he didn't really plan to record these songs, they were just something that he had to let out – a series of open musical letters to his wife.

When the group eventually got together to write, they decided to each bring a couple of songs and develop them as a band. Writing took place in Collins' house in Guilford where he was now living with house guest Robin Lumley of Brand X. The activities of the previous two years seem to have provided the creative juice that had been lacking to a certain extent across the last couple of releases, resulting in *Duke*. Banks commented in interviews that it was his favourite Genesis album, and all three have since remarked on how much easier, and more enjoyable the writing and recording process was, Rutherford adding that with only three in the band it was much easier to agree on a musical direction.

It was also the first release to give Collins a sole writing credit of any

Genesis material with two songs, 'Misunderstanding' and 'Please Don't Ask'. Coming off the back of the breakup of his marriage Collins had already written and recorded demos for *Face Value*, though it wasn't to be released until a year later. Indeed, at the time of writing for *Duke*, Collins wasn't even sure he could, or would release a solo album. He had played Banks and Rutherford the demos of several songs, and together the band chose those two songs for inclusion. Banks claims never to have heard 'In The Air Tonight', the famed massive hit from *Face Value*, as if he had it would have appeared on *Duke*, but Collins says he is pretty sure he played it to him at that time as he wasn't any more protective of that song than any of the others.

The 'Duke Suite' was a series of linked tracks scattered across the album. The original order was intended to be 'Behind The Lines', 'Duchess', 'Guide Vocal', 'Turn It On Again' (shorter version), 'Duke's Travels' and 'Duke's End', however the band felt that putting them together would invite comparisons to 'Supper's Ready'. The suite tells the story of Albert, our small headed moon gazer from the cover.

This was the last concerted progressive salvo by the band, even though more commercial material is included, such as the successful singles 'Turn It On Again' and 'Misunderstanding'. 'Alone Tonight', written by Rutherford, sounds like something that might have appeared on a Collins solo album and demonstrates elegantly how much his bandmate influenced Collins' writing style. It was not only pivotal in launching the band into their most commercially successful period but, coupled with *Face Value*, it became the springboard for Collins to achieve major solo success throughout the next few years. The tour which followed was a huge success, the band playing 70 dates over three months.

The cover was designed again by Hipgnosis with illustrations from Lionel Koechlin.

'Behind the Lines' 5:30 (Banks, Collins, Rutherford)
Duke starts with a rousing horn-like chord progression on keyboards, backed by multiple drum fills, bass pedals and soaring guitars. It was used as the opening piece on the 1981 *Abacab* tour, and later the introduction was also used to kick off the *Turn It On Again* shows in 2007. Another version would appear on the Phil Collins' *Face Value* a year later embellished with real horns and a Motown-style sound. Collins commented in the *Classic Albums* series that while recording that album the horn players played 'Behind The Lines' at double speed, and 'another song appeared'. It is a great way to open *Duke* with Banks paring back the arrangement for the verse with his Yamaha CP-70 grand piano played through a Boss chorus pedal, even using brass stabs which are here used with subtlety and work better than the ones he was to use later on the *Genesis* album. Rutherford's bassline is superb, and we are also treated to a wonderful Hackett-style solo towards the end.

'Duchess' 6:25 (Banks, Collins, Rutherford)

The song tells the story of the rise and fall of a female singer, 'Duchess'. From her early days dreaming of the adoration of the crowd, through the peak of her career when all she had to do was to step into the light to gain cheers, and finally in her decline when all she has left are her dreams. We hear the first use of a drum machine in a Genesis album throughout the song, a Roland CR-78 CompuRhythm with which Collins had been noodling. On the subsequent tour, he introduced this as another member of the band, Roland, the bi-sexual drum machine as 'he doesn't mind who he plays with'. This song was released as a single in May 1980 with 'Open Door' as the B-side. It failed to chart in the US but reached number 46 in the UK charts.

'Guide Vocal' 1:34 (Banks)

This is the shortest track on the album, but a personal favourite. It is a soulful, almost mournful piece telling how the Duke and Duchess have reached the end of their relationship, with each of the two verses relating how the one feels about the other. It has a simple, but hugely effective Yamaha piano combined with bass, and strings added in the second verse. Collins' vocal handles the emotion of this song exceptionally well, and it's a pity it was so short. However, it was clearly felt to be far too good to be used only once, and it is reprised in 'Duke's Travels' towards the end of the album.

'Man of Our Times' 5:35 (Rutherford)

This song is much rockier than the rest of Duke and feels a bit out of place in the sequencing of tracks on the album, leaving many to suspect it was leftover from Rutherford's solo album *Smallcreep's Day*. A heavy bass and synthesiser driven verse, leading into a grandiose, bass pedal-filled chorus. The treatment used on Collins' vocals creates a harsher tone in keeping with the style of the song. It is probably most memorable for introducing the 'tonight, tonight' motif that would later be re-worked on *Invisible Touch*.

'Misunderstanding' 3:14 (Collins)

Originally written by Collins as one of the songs for his solo album *Face Value*, the other band members liked it so much they wanted to use it on *Duke*. It is another song following the theme of the breakup of a relationship, and when released in August 1980 with 'Evidence Of Autumn' as the B-side in the UK, and 'Behind The Lines Part II' in the US, it was the best charting single so far for the band to that point in the US. It reached number fourteen in the *Billboard Hot 100* charts and 42 in the UK charts. It's a fun, doo-wop style pop song despite the downbeat lyrics, but nothing more.

'Heathaze' 5:00 (Banks)

This is another typical Banks ballad with a big chorus, although the lyrics seem to follow the romanticism of some of his songs on the previous two albums. The words seem to tell of sitting on a park bench on a warm sunny day, enjoying a cooling breeze and watching the world go by. Others are walking dogs, jogging, or passing their time, and he sits there feeling out of place 'I feel like an alien. A stranger in an alien place.'

'Turn It On Again' 3:51 (Banks, Collins, Rutherford)
This was the first, and most successful of the three singles to be taken from the album in the UK, released in May 1980 with 'Behind The Line Part II' as the B-side in the UK and ' Evidence Of Autumn' in the US, reaching number eight in the UK and 58 in the US. It tells how Duchess makes a comeback and reunites with Duke. Tonally, the song may sound like a standard pop song, yet it has a very odd 13/8 timing. The verse/chorus sections alternate time signatures, 6/4 to 7/4, while the intro and bridge sections are in 4/4 and 5/4. Rutherford remembers that he 'had this riff, but at the time it was played slower. And Phil said, 'Why don't you try it at a faster speed?' and then he said to me, 'Do you realise it is in 13/8?' And I said, 'What do you mean, it's in 13? It's in 4/4, isn't it?', 'No, it's 13' replied Collins. When Gabriel joined the band in 1982 for the one-off show *Six Of The Best*, he played the drums on this song while Collins sang, and found it very tricky to play.

'Alone Tonight' 3:57 (Rutherford)
This song continues the theme of the end of a relationship, even though Rutherford wrote it and would not have been out of place on *Face Value* both in terms of tone and style. It is another song indicative of the writing style both Rutherford and Banks were developing, towards shorter songs. Here a quiet verse is lifted by a big – even bombastic – chorus. Rutherford, particularly, develops further the songwriting style used on his earlier song 'Your Own Special Way'. The quiet guitar and vocal opening sets the introspective feel of the song, Collins clearly identifying with Rutherford's lyrics within the context of his own life. The chorus lifts the song with a full keyboard and drum arrangement, and the second short verse varies the arrangement by adding keyboards. Often overlooked, this song is a key step in the development of the band's overall song style and a significant forerunner of the hugely-successful pop/rock style they would achieve on later albums.

'Cul-de-Sac' 5:05 (Banks)
Very much a return to the style of *A Trick of the Tail* in both musical and lyrical style, this song details a hopeless battle in which there is no glory in pointless slaughter. The quiet vocal and piano opening gives way to a grandiose orchestral arrangement complete with timpani style drums. It is a strong prog-orientated number that stands up well against other gems such as 'Behind The Lines' and 'Dukes Travels'. However, it was never played

live, probably due to the multiple layers of keyboards used, where even a fairground pipe organ appears in the mix at one point, to reappear later at the end of 'Duke's Travels'. The ending is a feast of Banks chord progressions, before a quieter, but dramatic close.

'Please Don't Ask' 4:02 (Collins)
Written by Collins while developing ideas for *Face value*, this is another heartbreaker, a ballad about Collins' divorce and the awkward conversations that took place between the couple. The most heartwrenching lyric is 'But I miss my boy. Oh, I hope he's good as gold' – referring to Simon, his son, now a successful musician in his own right. Despite the melancholic lyrical content, the song builds to a relatively upbeat tempo as it develops.

'Duke's Travels' 8:39 (Banks, Collins, Rutherford)
The penultimate track in the Duke Suite is another bombastic, mainly instrumental piece with a reprise of 'Guide Vocal' towards the end. It's clear that when they were writing this piece, they were considering not only how the music would sit within the album, but how it would play out in a live set, with the big, anthemic and dramatic pieces always pleasing the audience in a live setting. Starting with a blanket multi-guitar, strumming texture before the drums start the track in earnest, Banks solos over most of the remaining six minutes as Collins provides the driving force behind it. A brief guitar solo brings us to the reprise of 'Guide Vocal', and here it is a triumphant version with a big arrangement. The final solo from Banks playing the 'Guide Vocal' melody is a fantastic way to start to break down the song which ends with a lone pipe organ playing a fairground theme that takes us straight into 'Duke's End'.

'Duke's End' 2:07 (Banks, Collins, Rutherford)
A reprise of 'Behind The Lines' kicks off this instrumental, running through a modified section of 'Turn It On Again' making for a fitting and satisfying conclusion to the album and bringing the 'Duke Suite' to a rousing end.

Related tracks
'Evidence of Autumn' 4:57 (Banks)
This track has a dark, brooding introduction from Banks on his ever-present Yamaha CP70 piano, while Collins sings this song with his quieter voice much like on *A Trick Of The Tail*. Overall, the song recalls 'Entangled' in tone, but with keyboards replacing guitars although the odd, bouncy instrumental break is a distraction from the otherwise consistently dark vibe of the song. During the chorus, background strings play something very like the guitar phrase used in the verse of 'Many Too Many'. The song was released in the UK as the B-side to 'Misunderstanding' in August 1980.

'Open Door' 4:06 (Rutherford)

'Open Door' is a real gem of a track, that was almost certainly left off the album due to its similarity in style to 'Alone Tonight', but is actually a much more accomplished song and arrangement than the better-known song. The simple arrangement of acoustic guitar, piano, strings and synthesised woodwinds perfectly back the plaintive vocal from Collins. The song was released as the B-side of 'Duchess' in May 1980.

Abacab (1981)

Personnel:
Tony Banks: keyboards
Phil Collins: drums, vocals
Mike Rutherford: basses, guitars
Recorded at The Farm, Surrey between May and June 1981
Producer: Genesis
Sleeve design: Bill Smith
Released: 18 September 1981 in the UK, 24 September 1981 in the US
Label: Charisma, Atlantic
Highest Chart places: UK: 1, US: 7. Achieved double platinum in the US (1,000,000)
and gold in the UK (100,000), France (50,000) and Germany (100,000).
Running time: 47:10

So, we now come to *Abacab*. At the time, this was the start of my self-imposed
Genesis hiatus. It would be the first release since *Foxtrot* that I didn't rush out and
buy on the day of release having already heard 'Abacab' and 'No Reply At All' which
were released as singles before the album. I have never subscribed to the school
of thought that Collins' move to vocals destroyed Genesis, *A Trick of the Tail* and
Duke being in my top five albums from the band. Nor do I believe progressive
bands should not 'progress', it was just that in this instance, the direction of
progression didn't suit me personally. 'Hate' is a very strong and often misused
word, but I'd go as far as saying that at the time I hated *Abacab*, I felt cheated, my
favourite band in the world had tried something new, changed direction, and left
me lying at the side of the road licking my progressive wounds.

Isn't it amazing, though, what almost 40 years and a lot of hindsight can do?
I still can't say it's great, but I can now listen to it in the context of where this
step ultimately took Genesis. This is the one I have wrestled with and come
back to, more than any other during the writing of this book in an attempt to
ensure I give it a fair hearing. Despite another UK number one, and US double
platinum, Abacab was seen by many as a poor follow up to Duke both in terms
of the quality and memorability of the music. This view is borne out by its
longevity in later tours, with only 'Abacab' and 'Dodo' ever making it to the
setlist beyond the Abacab tour. After the Invisible Touch tour, which featured
'Abacab', nothing was ever played live from it again.

However, Rutherford says that they had to change or die; without change, he
would have gotten bored years previously, Banks adding:

*Abacab often provokes a strange response, but it was an absolutely
necessary album in our career. We had to change – we couldn't carry on
as we were. It marked a watershed.*

The band had decided to cut back on complexity, solos and big choruses,
exactly the area that endeared the band to many of their existing fans. It

wasn't necessarily an attempt to make a more commercial release, but certainly a desire to break with the patterns of the past. Banks reports wanting to create something more abstract, an album to the other extreme of the romanticism and complexity of *Wind & Wuthering*. Every instrumental part was questioned as to its right to be included, paring down the arrangements to a minimum. The drums are very much to the fore on this album, with keyboards almost disappearing into the background in places. The title of the album comes from the original structure of the title song which was ABACAB, where A is the verse, B the chorus, C the bridge, and was an easy way to remember it as they worked the track up, according to Collins. During development, the structure of the song changed and would have become unpronounceable using the same naming structure, but the original title remained.

Despite the amount of effort the band put into the release – by this time they had their own studio – at the time I felt the album was lazy, with poor songs and few redeeming features. At best, it is an experiment that yielded few positive results, but now it is clear that this approach was required as a first step in the progression towards Invisible Touch. Listening to the album again, I still found myself shaking my head and shouting at the stereo, 'how could you, this is utter tosh! Which impostor is playing keyboards, and what have you done with Tony Banks?' However, during recording, every note was questioned as to whether it was needed, leading to a minimalist arrangement on most songs. Today, I still view this album as one of the poorest releases from the band and feel that in their desire to adapt and minimise their sound, the band simply discarded the momentum and consistency gained with *Duke*. I understand many fans, particularly those who discovered the band at this time, rate Abacab highly, so you may want to skip to the 1983 release *Genesis* with my heartfelt apologies.

Of the nine tracks, six were credited to the group, the other three credited to one member each. 'Me And Sarah Jane' from Banks, 'Man On The Corner' from Collins and 'Like It Or Not' from Rutherford. Collins recalls that when playing two dates in October 1981 at Groenoordhallen in Leiden, Holland, the crowd booed every *Abacab* track the band played.

This was the first Genesis album record at The Farm, a 24-track studio the band had built in the cowshed of an old farm in Chiddingfold, Surrey. They had purchased it to convert it to a studio for their sole use for both writing and recording. The album was also self-produced, the first and only time they would record without another producer in the studio, although they did bring in Hugh Padgham to help engineer the album and he who would go on to produce the next two. The title song was written in the living room of the house, Collins remarking that it was the first time they had talked and worked together as a team.

It was during the time of writing *Abacab* that Collins' *Face Value* was topping charts around the world, and 'In The Air Tonight' was number one in the singles charts in several countries. Banks says in the 2014 documentary *Genesis: Together and Apart*:

We wanted Phil to do well. Just not that well.

Although there was more than enough material recorded for a double album at the time, the band decided to abandon anything that sounded like their previous material. Three of those tracks were released later on the *3x3* extended play single.

Bill Smith designed the cover, and an undefinable shape was chosen as the main motif to match that abstract aim of the material. Not only were there four different versions of the cover, all with different colour schemes released, but the Genesis logo was replaced by one hand-drawn in pencil. No lyrics were included in the packaging, as Banks wanted to reduce the emphasis on the words, believing they had been overemphasised on previous releases.

'Abacab' 6:57 (Banks, Collins, Rutherford)

The album-opening is promising, with an up-front drum sound, pounding bass and exciting keyboard stabs. However, the verse and chorus are short of ideas with poor lyrics, and later the song wanders into a somewhat bland jam session. Genesis often wrote some of their best music through jamming – most of *The Lamb* was written this way – but they usually picked the best parts of those jams and developed them. This jam is just poor. As a live track, however, the song came into its own, especially during the *Invisible Touch* tour. In the rehearsal footage for 2007's *Turn It On Again: The Tour*, Collins says halfway through the first verse of 'Abacab' that he really didn't want to sing it, as he had no idea what the song was all about.

The song was released as the first single from the album on 14 August 1981 in the UK, with 'Another Record' as the B-side. It peaked at number 26 in the US and nine in the UK. The UK single version was slightly longer than the US version, at 4:10, compared with 3:59.

'No Reply at All' 4:39 (Banks, Collins, Rutherford)

The Phoenix horn section from Earth Wind And Fire, who had helped create the distinctive sound of Collins' solo albums, were brought in to play on this song, which is reminiscent of 'Missed Again' from *Face Value*. The line 'Is anyone listening? No reply at all' sums up how I felt about *Abacab* at the time. The song is notable as the first Genesis song to feature guest musicians since the string section on *From Genesis To Revelation* – the only other time would be on the last album *Calling All Stations* where two guest drummers would be used. Collins has commented, quite bitterly about the decision to bring in the horn section, saying:

Why not have horns on it, who says we can't have horns on it, it's our fucking record, you know. So, we did it, and people hated it.

This was the second single from the album, released on 9 September 1981 with 'Naminanu' and 'Dodo' as the B-side. It reached number 29 in the *US Billboard 100* but failed to chart in the UK. I certainly enjoy it a lot more than I ever did at the time.

'Me and Sarah Jane' 5:59 (Banks)
Banks brings us one of his renowned chord fests in this song, written before the band gathered to work on the album, so it sounds more like previous material before the mantra of simplicity became the daily chant of the band. It starts slowly with a drum machine pattern, and the simplistic staccato playing style from Banks feels somewhat uncomfortable, but the song quickly opens up after the tempo change at 0:55. The verse jogs along until a long chord progression takes us to an uplifting section at 3:11. It feels like we were now at the best part of the song, but once again Banks takes us up a level at 3:30, and once again at 4:05 and these last sections are spectacular. Even as the end of the piece fades out, Banks throws in a few new chords just for good measure. Banks has since commented:

I poured all this flowery stuff into one song and reminded myself to keep it simple on the rest of the album. It is probably my last Genesis song that had thousands of those chord changes.

'Keep It Dark' 4:31 (Banks, Collins, Rutherford)
While playing a riff as a band, one section including the guitar and drums was taken and looped throughout the track which makes it drag somewhat, only pausing for a few seconds for Collins to play what sounds like some kitchen pots and bottles and sing 'Keep It Dark', before returning to the loop. Given there were numerous benefits to writing much of the album together in the studio, such as a freer, less prescriptive style and a more supportive, collaborative sound, this song exposes one of the drawbacks. With an eagerness to adopt new technology, but without the time to tame and bottle it, tedium is created around the overuse of the rhythm loop. Even though having their own studio removed much of the time pressure to create, I'm sure given more time to develop an idea like this without peer pressure within the band would have resulted in a modified – or even, dare I say, no – version of this song being recorded.

The song is the story of a person who is abducted by aliens and sees many fantastic sights, but on his return can't tell anyone as he fears that they wouldn't believe him. It was the third single from the album, released on 23 October 1981 with 'Naminanu' again as its B-side. It reached number 33 in the UK but failed to chart in the US.

'Dodo / Lurker' 7:29 (Banks, Collins, Rutherford)
This is the best track on the album so far, starting with a huge keyboard chord blast and soaring lead guitar. The song moves through several sections

with Collins singing one of them in a lower register making him almost unrecognisable. The lyrics are written from the perspective of someone who is not a native English speaker. The solo from Banks in the 'Lurker' section when Collins sings 'and then something spoke, and this is what it said to me' is very simple but it works beautifully in the context of the song.

'Who Dunnit?' 3:24 (Banks, Collins, Rutherford)

I really should heed my Mother's advice that 'If you can't say anything nice, keep your mouth shut!', but my job is to review every album, every track, even this one. This, apparently, was the band's attempt at a punk-style song. Even Banks admits that many see this as the worst song the band ever recorded and says that the lyric was as irritating as the music. We agree on both points. I really have a hard time getting through to the end of this song, especially when the vocal loops start, even now.

'Man on the Corner' 4:25 (Collins)

The only track credited individually to Collins, even though other tracks obviously had a lot of 'Collins' in them. A drum machine pattern is used again, but this time it works well. Rutherford says it was tricky getting the timing right to spot the upbeat when to come in when playing on top of it. It has a nice, simple keyboard pad through the verse but the song opens up halfway through when the drums come in, and the mood lifts. It's a song I liked when it was released, and it still has a lot of charm now.

After a gap of five months since 'Keep It Dark' had been released, this would be the fourth single from the album released on 5 March 1982 with 'Submarine' as the B-side. It peaked at number 40 in the US and 41 in the UK.

'Like It or Not' 4:52 (Rutherford)

Another song with a simple, slow, swing beat the opening of this song is reminiscent of 'Misunderstanding'. Rutherford was always a good writer of short, catchy, commercial songs even before the formation of his other band Mike and The Mechanics and the track is only let down by the use of the saxophone synth 'solo' by Banks. It would have been much better with a more standard synth sound, or even – dare I say it – an actual sax player.

'Another Record' 4:20 (Banks, Collins, Rutherford)

Finally, the keyboard-playing imposter is ejected from the studio and Banks returns for the last song with some great Yamaha piano and lush synth pad in the introduction, leading into what sadly becomes another drum-heavy track. The chorus, which tells the listener to put another record on, seems very appropriate at this point. Even the short, perky, Beatles-style middle eight can't redeem the rather dull song. And yes, that's a keyboard-generated faux harmonica you can hear.

Related Tracks
There were at least five fully recorded tracks from the *Abacab* sessions which did not make the album. Three would be released as the *3x3* EP, and the other two would be released as B-sides.

'Submarine' 4:38 (Banks, Collins, Rutherford)
This piece is an instrumental with a lush wall of keyboards. It is rather more laid back than any of the tracks which made it onto *Abacab* and is very much in the style of Pink Floyd's 'Shine On You Crazy Diamond'. I really like this piece, though it sounds like it would have made a fitting section to a longer song, as it doesn't really go anywhere on its own and is left unresolved. There is speculation on several Genesis forums of a possible 'Dodo Suite' that ran as, 'Dodo/Lurker', 'Submarine' then 'Naminanu', with the last two dropped from the final album. It does make some sense, but to my knowledge, there has never been any confirmation of this by the band. It was released as the B-side of the 'Man on the Corner' single.

'Naminanu' 3:52 (Banks, Collins, Rutherford)
This is another instrumental with a nonsense lyrical refrain, basically 'Naminanu' repeated. Genesis would often rehearse with a word or words that worked phonetically before the final lyrics were written. In this case, no words were ever penned. It is less memorable than 'Submarine', and it was certainly the correct decision to leave it off the album. It was released as the B-side of 'Keep It Dark'.

3x3 EP
Personnel:
Tony Banks: keyboards
Phil Collins: drums, percussion, vocals
Mike Rutherford: guitars, bass
Recorded at The Farm, Surrey between May and June 1981
Producer: Genesis
Released: 21 May 1982
Sleeve design: Back cover and liner notes by Tony Barrow
Label: Charisma
Highest Chart places: UK:10, US: Not released. Achieved silver in the UK (60,000) and gold in Germany (100,000)
Running time: 15:08

Three tracks that were recorded during the *Abacab* sessions were released as an EP in the UK. The cover had a photo of the three band members jumping in the air in a pastiche of the cover of The Beatles 1963 EP 'Twist And Shout', something they would try again later with the 'Land Of Confusion' single from *Invisible Touch*.

The back cover and liner notes were designed by Tony Barrow who had designed that Beatles cover. The three tracks would appear later that year on side four of the original international (non-UK) release of *Three Sides Live*. The EP stands up well as a short selection of songs, and it is certainly easier to listen to than *Abacab*.

The EP peaked at number ten in the UK. In the US 'Paperlate' was released as a standard single on 15 May 1982 with 'You Might Recall' as the B-side, peaking at number 32 in the US charts.

'Paperlate' 3:20 (Banks, Collins, Rutherford)
Another track that used the Phoenix Horns to create a 60s soul vibe, this track had previously been released as the B-side to 'Tonight, Tonight, Tonight'. The title came from 'Dancing With The Moonlit Knight', 'Paper late, cried a voice in the crowd'. It was a straight choice between this and 'No Reply At All' for the album as they are similar, beyond the use of the horns.

'You Might Recall' 5:30 (Banks, Collins, Rutherford)
This is a better song than most that are on *Abacab*. Rutherford says this is reminiscent of 'Alone Tonight' and 'Say It's Alright Joe', though it is more upbeat than either of those songs. Collins' drumming is great on this, and the only disappointment is Banks' selection of a twee, squeaky patch for the short solo. The fade out at the end of the song seems to start mid-verse as if they gave up on the end the song.

'Me and Virgil' 6:18 (Banks, Collins, Rutherford)
Collins calls the song 'a dog' and cites this as the worst example of his songwriting, and I have to agree with him. Such was his dislike for the song; it was omitted from the *Genesis Archive Two: 1976 – 1992* release which included the other two tracks from this EP. The song was, however, included in the box set *Genesis 1976-1982* with the other two tracks from the EP.

Genesis (1983)

Personnel:
Tony Banks: keyboards, backing vocals
Mike Rutherford: guitars, bass guitars, backing vocals
Phil Collins: drums, percussion, lead vocals
Recorded at the Farm
Producer: Genesis and Hugh Padgham
Sleeve design: Bill Smith Studios
Released: 4 October 1983
Label: Charisma/Virgin in the UK and Atlantic in the US
Highest Chart places: UK: 1, US: 9. Reached number 1 in Germany and achieved quadruple platinum in the US (4,000,000), double platinum in the UK (600,000) and platinum in France (100,000) and Germany (200,000).
Running time: 45:59

Genesis was another UK number one album, and a number nine in the US, just shy of the number seven that *Abacab* achieved. Five singles were released from the album, 'Mama' reaching number four in the UK in September 1983, which was to be their highest chart position for a single in the UK. The album was a return to better form in some ways, as evidenced by the sales figures. In particular, this was the album that really started the band's turnaround in fortunes in the singles chart, with 'That's All' peaking at number six and in terms of sales, *Genesis* was a major jump from *Abacab,* despite its lower peak in the US album charts. Overall, it sold twice as many units as *Abacab* in the USA and six times as many copies in the UK, achieving multiple awards, including quadruple platinum in the US, which is awarded over 4,000,000 copies, an astonishing performance.

This was the first album that was written, recorded and mixed in the studio at The Farm, *Abacab* having been written in the main house while the studio was being built in the cowshed. It was also the first album to be recorded without the members of the band bringing in any pre-written ideas or complete songs to the studio. The whole album was written collaboratively from scratch by the three members of the band, hence the eponymous title of the album. The credits for each song simply show 'Genesis' rather than being named after each group member, as had been the convention for several albums previously. It is sometimes called the 'Shapes' album, or even 'Mama', and as a result of this new approach to writing, there was only just enough material recorded to complete the album at just over 45 minutes with no additional tracks recorded for B-sides.

It is so fitting that Banks likens *Abacab* to clearing out all the furniture from a room, and *Genesis* as the redecorating. This view is certainly true when it comes to the arrangements, and the evidence of a return to a somewhat richer, more complex sonic palate and *Genesis* remains Rutherford's favourite Genesis album. Two recent technological innovations were used to good effect with Collins playing the latest Simmons digital drum kit, and Banks playing the Emulator sampler keyboard, using it to create many of the new sounds used on the album. Hugh Padgham was brought in to work with the band on production having worked with Collins on *Face Value*, and *Hello, I Must Be Going*, and his work would continue with *Invisible Touch*. The benefits of his production work on Collins' drums are clear with a much fuller, dominant and driving sound.

Bill Smith Studios designed the album cover. The shapes in the cover photo are from a 'Shape O', a Tupperware child's toy which featured a red and blue ball into which the yellow shapes could be inserted through matching holes. The Genesis logo here was a simple script font.

'Mama' 6:47 (Genesis)

The Highest charting single from Genesis in the UK was released on 3 September 1983 with 'It's Gonna Get Better' as the B-side, reaching number four. More than any other this song by the band, it highlights the difference in the popular music trends across the Atlantic as it didn't fare anywhere near so well in the US when it was released on 22 August 1983, only peaking at number 73, the poppier, more conventional single 'That's All' faring much better. 'Mama' is a dark, brooding number that builds perfectly over a looped electronic rhythm. Once again Genesis start an album with a new, challenging sound, ousting any temptation to stand still or repeat what had already been done. Banks used an ARP Quadra linked over MIDI to the Linn drum machine, with the hi-hat rhythm triggering the chords to create the 16th note vamping effect. Possibly inspired by the simplicity of the drums and bass, Banks manages to keep this keyboard parts and solos simple, but achieves a more direct performance, playing fewer notes than he might have in the 1970s, but all perfectly selected and in the right place. While the power of the song is evident on the studio version, once again, like 'Abacab', it is the live version that defines 'Mama' as a classic Genesis song of the Collins era. Along with 'Home by the Sea' it featured in every tour set after the album's release, including *Calling All Stations* and the 2007 Reunion Tour. The lyrics were written by Collins, about a young man's infatuation with an older prostitute. He has an Oedipus complex and calls her 'Mama'. In an interview, Collins said that the story was inspired by *The Moon's a Balloon*, David Niven's autobiography in which he tells the story of leaving cadet school and falling for an older lady of the night. The laughing in the song is supposedly based on Grandmaster Flash's song 'The Message', released in 1982, though it feels more caricature than imitation.

During interviews at the time of the album re-issues, Rutherford says he was experimenting with a Linn drum machine played through a gated reverb into a small mesa boogie amplifier turned up incredibly loud, so much so that the amplifier was jumping up and down on the chair. This provided the muffled bass drum and gunshot snare sound used in the looped rhythm. Steve Hackett says that this is his favourite Genesis number released after he left the band, describing it as 'beautifully haunting'.

'That's All' 4:26 (Genesis)

This was the song that really started the pop career for Genesis, particularly in the USA. It is a simple, radio-friendly, Beatles-like song with a traditional verse-chorus format. It is, of course, typical of Genesis to do this sort of thing differently, and here the twist is that both a keyboard and a guitar solo are featured. Opening with piano and a simple beat that Collins describes as his attempt on a Ringo Starr drum part, the song is a great example of how the band could now channel their writing into a simpler, shorter and ultimately more commercial, direction. Even the solos from Banks and Rutherford are simplified and generally follow the main melody, reinforcing the hook lines, perfect for such an instantly-likeable pop song. 'That's All' was released with 'Second Home by the Sea' as the B-side when it was released in the US on 3 October 1983, and with 'Taking It All Too Hard' as the B-side when released on 12 November 1983 in the UK. It gave the band their first US top ten single, reaching number six, and reached number sixteen in the UK charts. When a 12-inch version was released, the B-side was a live version of 'Firth Of Fifth' from 1981, almost the antithesis of 'That's All'. This may have been a smart marketing ploy by the band's management to continue to appeal to the progressive fanbase while at the same time developing a more mainstream audience.

'Home by the Sea' 4:52 (Genesis)

The lyrics for this song feature an idea from Banks about a burglar breaking into an old house only to find it haunted, hearing the words 'Welcome to the home by the sea'. He is then imprisoned in the house while the ghosts tell their story 'Sit down, sit down, as we relive our lives in what we tell you.' and 'Sit down, sit down, cause you won't get away'. Bank's use of haunting keyboard pads with spooky sound effects creates a great atmosphere in the song, though the idea for the lyrics came after the mood and sound of the track had been developed, with Collins singing the line 'Home by the sea' over and over during the writing sessions, inspiring Banks to write this seaside ghost story. This was such a band and audience favourite that along with 'Second Home by the Sea' and 'Mama' it was played on every subsequent tour.

'Second Home by the Sea' 6:22 (Genesis)

The instrumental section, tagged onto 'Home by the Sea', was developed in a couple of two-hour jam sessions with the best sections being used on the final track. Simmons electronic drum sounds are used throughout the piece, with Banks soloing over a heavy keyboard and guitar backing. It is quite simple, but it's hugely effective and became a great song to play live. After an opening section that hints at the promise of things to come, the changes at 1:19 and again at 3:24 are inspired, elevating the track to something much more interesting than was first apparent. Towards the end, the song quietens to allow Collins the space to reprise a verse from the previous song, before it fades. It was released as the B-side to the US version of 'That's All'.

'Illegal Alien' 5:15 (Genesis)

Side two starts with 'Illegal Alien' and immediately the opening few bars of car horns and the odd opening riff indicate this is something completely different from any of the previous four tracks from the first side of the album and another odd departure for the band. It was meant to be a light-hearted song about illegal aliens in the USA, with Collins singing in an awful, mock Hispanic accent. As a song, it's certainly indicative of its time and the significant difference in social and political correctness compared with today – you could not release such a single now without a serious backlash. I am no lover of this track, in fact pretty much everything about it is annoying, from the Collins' accent to the choice of instruments, and the lyrics – what was Rutherford thinking when he wrote 'I've got a sister who'd be willing to oblige. She will do anything now to get me to the outside'? Following years of not hearing it, my enforced listening for this book highlighted the earworm that is the chorus, which echoes around the head for an uncomfortable amount of time afterwards. At a time when radio play was often based more on the overall sound, and less on misheard or even overlooked lyrics, I can now see how it broke into the top 50 on both sides of the Atlantic. The song was released as a single with a live version of 'Turn It On Again' as the B-side in the US on 23 January 1984, although it only reached number 44, similarly reaching number 46 when released in the UK on 11 February 1984. As mentioned, Mike Rutherford wrote the lyrics, giving it the working title 'Mexican Tourist Board' or 'MTB'. At the time, Banks defended the song against claims of racism, saying it was supposed to be tongue in cheek and was meant to be sympathetic towards illegal aliens.

'Taking It All Too Hard' 3:58 (Genesis)

This is another experiment in concise, commercial songwriting, but in this case, it is one that works very well. Electing to go straight in with the chorus rather than the verse, it looks to grab the listeners attention as quickly as possible with the often-misheard chorus lyric of 'You're taking it all to heart, you're taking it all too hard'. Rutherford wrote the words and says he was trying to write a love song but admits that while the words sounded good within the context of the song, they didn't necessarily make much sense, a throwback to a trick that Gabriel used on the earlier albums. Sonically, the selection of percussive keyboard sounds gives the chorus an almost Caribbean feel, with very rich backing vocals. The upbeat chorus is contrasted by a more restrained verse which is needed to help carry lyrics such as 'But I still miss you. I keep it to myself'. Once again we can hear elements, particularly in the chorus, that were the stepping stones towards 'Invisible Touch'. The song was released as a single in the US only, in June 1984 with 'Silver Rainbow' as the B-side. It was the last single released from the album, peaking at 50 on the *Billboard 100*, although it got to eleven on the adult contemporary chart.

'Just a Job to Do' 4:47 (Genesis)

This is very much a track rooted in the 80s with its keyboard brass stabs, muted guitar and vocal stylisations (e.g. 'Bang Bang') and general similarity to the sonic tonality of the time. This guitar driven track tells of a hitman who receives no more than a name and a number to identify his next target, making it 'just a job to do'. No doubt in response to the backlash against the use of real horns on *Abacab,* Banks chose again to use keyboard horns, although, ironically, this song would have worked better had the Phenix Horns been involved. The introduction and verse are based around a great guitar and bass riff that, at first, sounds deceptively simple but is actually quite intricately constructed. The chorus is strong and punchy, but it is the break at 2:24 that begins with 'Keep running, keep running' that provides the highlight and a welcome change of tempo before returning to the last verse and chorus. It was the only song from the album not to be released on a single, either as an A or B-side.

'Silver Rainbow' 4:29 (Genesis)

By this point in the album, 'Silver Rainbow' serves to highlight the diversity of the styles adopted on *Genesis.* Is it inconsistency rather than diversity? The whole second side of the album is often dismissed by hardcore fans, including myself at the time, preferring side one for it's more traditional, simplified prog style. However, those that do miss out on this little gem. Banks weaves an intricate texture of samples through the introduction to create a complex rhythm with Collins' distant vocal declaring 'Rivers flow uphill, blue turns to grey. Winter follows springtime; morning ends the day', something that can only happen in another world beyond the 'Silver Rainbow'. Amazingly, for one song, we are back in the 'elf and goblin' territory of fantastical lyrics. The verse is based around a simple piano pattern, leading into a strong, catchy, keyboard-based chorus. The mix is almost devoid of any guitar, but the song works as a throwback to earlier styles and is the only hint of progressive music on the second side of the album. The song was released as the B- side to 'Taking It All Too Hard' in the US only.

'It's Gonna Get Better' 4:58 (Genesis)

This song is a simple but effective ballad about hope in hard times. The lush, backwards-sounding keyboard pad use at the start and during the song – a sample from a classical piano piece – is a delight. Banks wanted to capture a decent sample of strings, but when he played four notes together, the phasing of the different playback speeds accidentally created this great sound. Choosing to start with a chorus as they had done with 'Taking It All Too Hard', a single verse and chorus follows, plus a short reprise of the intro and a fantastic break at 3:27, with hints of 'Throwing It All Away,' that could have been even more effectively used as a strong chorus. When the extended twelve-inch mix was created, an additional verse and chorus were added before the short instrumental section before the break. For an even better version, listen to the one recorded live at the LA Forum in 1984 that is included on the *Genesis Archive #2 (1976-1992)* compilation which uses the extra verse to create a more satisfying ending with Collins riffing over a newly added guitar solo. The song was released as the B-side to 'Mama' on both the original and 12-inch versions.

Invisible Touch (1986)

Personnel:
Tony Banks: keyboards, synth bass
Phil Collins: drums, lead vocals, percussion, drum machine
Mike Rutherford: guitars, bass guitar
Recorded at The Farm, Surrey between October 1985 and February 1986
Producer: Genesis and Hugh Padgham
Mastered: By Bob Ludwig at Masterdisk New York City
Sleeve design: Baker Dave at Assorted Images with photos from John Swannell
Released: June 6 1986 in the US, June 9 1986 in the UK
Label: Charisma/Virgin in the UK and Atlantic in the US
Highest Chart places: UK: 1, US: 3. Achieved six times platinum in the US
(6,000,000), quadruple platinum in the UK (1,200,000) and platinum in France
(100,000) and Germany (200,000).
Running time: 45:43

Invisible Touch was to be the biggest selling Genesis album, grossing double that of *Genesis* in the UK, and 50% more in the US. It sold over six million copies in that territory alone, introducing a whole new generation to the band.

The trio regrouped after a break of almost two years, allowing time for more solo projects. Collins had now released three solo albums, the latest being *No Jacket Required* and had recently completed an 85-date world tour over five months, making him a hugely successful solo artist in his own right. Rutherford had formed Mike and The Mechanics, releasing their first eponymously titled album and had already achieved two top ten hits in the UK with 'Silent Running' and 'All I Need Is A Miracle'. Banks had worked on the soundtracks for two movies, *Quicksilver* and *Lorca and the Outlaws*, and had just released some of the music from them on his *Soundtracks* album. He also worked with vocalists Fish, Jim Diamond and Toyah Willcox for some additional tracks. Given that Banks was so integral to the band and the only irreplaceable member (according to manager Tony Smith), his level of solo success was much more modest than the other two. As with *Genesis*, the band wrote the material from scratch at the Farm, with no ideas or songs being brought to the rehearsals.

Given how inventive many of the band's albums had been, when *Invisible Touch* was released, by comparison it feels like a poor album, choosing to focus on the simpler, more commercial aspects of the music developed through *Abacab* and *Genesis*. At the time, even the longer tracks 'Tonight, Tonight, Tonight' and 'Domino' did little to spark my enthusiasm but it was later, when these songs were performed live, that they came into their own and I could finally appreciate them along side the rest of the band's back catalogue.

Indeed, *Invisible Touch* received mixed reviews, at best being considered a 'three out of five' album and was likened by critics to Collins' commercial solo work. This, of course, once again shows that critics and fans don't always agree. The album is hugely accessible, providing a gateway for many new fans to explore the band's previous work. Certainly, if commercial success was what the band were after, then this was definitely what they got. The band could do no wrong, particularly in the US, where five singles were released, a number one, two number threes and two number fours, spending a total of 86 weeks in the US charts. They became the first overseas band to have five top five singles in the US from the one album, with only three songs on the album not released as singles. Despite this phenomenal level of success, the album failed to reach number one in the US charts, peaking at number three, when, ironically, Peter Gabriel's *So* was at number two – the *Top Gun* soundtrack being at number one. To give some context to this, it was a year when Whitney Houston's debut album spent almost four months at number one, only interrupted from that position for three weeks by Van Halen's 5150. Genesis spent almost a year promoting the album on a 112-date world tour, ending with four sold-out nights at Wembley Stadium in London, which were filmed for a live video release.

The album received dubious praise in the 2000 movie *American Psycho*. The film is seen as a satire on the vacuity of the 1980s, partially via the main character – serial killer Patrick Bateman, played by Christian Bale – and is mentioned in the notorious scene where he critiques the album in the company of two prostitutes. Here we reproduce his speech in full, minus his rather more sexual asides to the two ladies in question:

Do you like Phil Collins? I've been a big Genesis fan ever since the release of their 1980 album, Duke. Before that, I really didn't understand any of their work. Too artsy, too intellectual. It was on Duke where Phil Collins' presence became more apparent, I think. I think Invisible Touch is the group's undisputed masterpiece. It's an epic meditation on intangibility. At the same time, it deepens and enriches the meaning of the preceding three albums. Listen to the brilliant ensemble playing of Banks, Collins and Rutherford. You can practically hear every nuance of every instrument. In terms of lyrical craftsmanship, the sheer songwriting, this album hits a new peak of professionalism. Take the lyrics to 'Land of Confusion'. In this song, Phil Collins addresses the problems of abusive political authority. 'In Too Deep' is the most moving pop song of the 1980s, about monogamy and commitment. The song is extremely uplifting. Their lyrics are as positive, affirmative, as anything I've heard in rock.

However, with hindsight, the criticisms and comparisons with Collins' solo work, including my own at the time, were somewhat overplayed. It is hard for Phil Collins not to sound like Phil Collins, and the more commercial nature of the music on this album was always going to appeal to mainstream Collins fans far more than any of the earlier band's material would have. Rutherford was also enjoying solo success in the singles charts at this time, so the combination of both musicians was always likely to lead to more commercial material from the band. That said, there were still more complex arrangements around some of the songs than Collins or Rutherford would have had on their solo releases, and 'Domino' was to provide a solid audience favourite for years to come. That said, it was another release that caused many long-term, devoted fans to vote with their wallets and not buy it, but their voices were lost in the huge influx of new fans. While so many refer to the Gabriel and Collins era of the band, I always think that in reality there were two Collins eras – pre and post-Abacab, and Invisible Touch was the commercial peak of that final period.

There were three additional songs recorded at the time, 'Do The Neurotic' which was the B-side to 'In Too Deep', 'Feeding The Fire' which was the B-side to 'Land Of Confusion' and 'I'd Rather Be you' which was the B-side to 'Throwing It All Away'. The cover design was by Dave Baker, aka Baker Dave of Assorted Images and once again the Genesis logo was replaced with a simple type font on this album.

'Invisible Touch' 3:26 (Banks, Collins, Rutherford)
From the first bars, we realise that once again this is a new Genesis sound. What started with *Abacab* and developed further with *Genesis,* had now reached its logical conclusion with a clever, but straightforward, pop song with a great hook. The first of five singles from the album, it became the first and only number one hit single from the band. Released on 19 May 1986 in the US with 'The Last Domino' as the B-side, it topped the US for one week only on 19 July 1992. Interestingly, number two that week was Peter Gabriel with 'Sledgehammer', the highest position his own singles achieved in the USA. It was released on 31 May 1986 in the UK, reaching number fifteen in the charts. A live version would later be released in November 1992 which would reach number seven in the UK.

'Tonight, Tonight, Tonight' 8:49 (Banks, Collins, Rutherford)
This song is about a meeting with a cocaine dealer and drug withdrawal symptoms. Clearly, Michelob knew none of this when they chose to use it in a high-profile advertising campaign in 1986 called 'The night belongs to Michelob' and sponsored the Genesis North American tour. It was, however, the spark that made the song a hit and released as a single on 23 March 1987, it reached number three in the US charts. It was also released on 14 March 1987 in the UK and reached number eighteen. The song has a slow build with multiple layers of drum machine, real drums and keyboard patterns. The keyboards play a simple chord pad, combined with a bass pedal drone. Somewhat surprisingly, the album that brought Genesis their biggest commercial success, also included two long songs with almost twenty of the albums 45 minutes accounted for from this and 'Domino'. The video for the single was filmed at the Bradbury Building in Los Angeles and recreated some of the scenes from *Blade Runner* which was filmed at the same location.

'Land of Confusion' 4:45 (Banks, Collins, Rutherford)

Released as a single in the UK on 22 November 1986, with 'Feeding The Fire' as the B-side, it reached number fourteen in the UK charts. When it was released later, on 31 January 1987, in the US, it reached number four. The music was written by the band with lyrics by Rutherford, about the abuse of power by those that hold it, highlighted in the supporting video created by the producers of *Spitting Image*, a UK satirical sketch show that used foam caricature puppets of famous figures from the worlds of entertainment, sports, politics and even British royalty. Collins had already featured as a puppet on the show, so he had the makers produce puppets for the other band members. Notable parts of the video show Rutherford on a four-neck guitar, and two Collins puppets, one on drums, the other singing and Banks surrounded by keyboards, and a cash register full of cookies. The video won the group their only Grammy in 1988 for 'Best Concept Music Video', and this is Banks' favourite video, particularly as the band didn't need to do anything in the filming of it. The cover of the single used the puppet heads of the band in a pastiche of the cover of The Beatles' second album *With The Beatles* from 1963, a trick they had tried previously with the *3x3* EP. This song – making use of the accompanying video – would be used to open the set on the *We Can't Dance tour* in 1992.

Rutherford's 'protest song', based around a couple of memorable guitar riffs, is a straightforward rock number and was 'easy to play' according to Banks. The guitar riff on the verses hints very strongly at the sort of line that Hackett would have written ten years earlier – a subtle blast from the past. The softer section about halfway through, with the 'I remember long ago' lyric provides a much-needed break from the relentless, pounding bass which would have become wearing had it continued throughout the song. It probably isn't the best of the band's hits, but it might just be most memorable, and the ultra-catchy 'oh, oh, oh' hook in the chorus would probably have made this a hit, even without the terrific video.

'In Too Deep' 4:59 (Banks, Collins, Rutherford)

Released as a single in the UK on 30 August 1986, with 'Do The Neurotic' as the B-side, 'In Too Deep' reached number nineteen in the UK charts. It wasn't released in the US until 18 January 1987 and reached number three. Collins wrote the lyrics after being approached to write a song for the 1986 movie *Mona Lisa* with Bob Hoskins, for which Genesis won a BAFTA for 'Most Performed Song from a Film'. It was also used on the soundtrack of the movie *American Psycho* in 2000.

The song is the big romantic ballad on the album and the track that sounds most like Collins' solo work. The lush tones of Banks' keyboards, the understated guitar, big drums and smooth vocal highlight the quality of the production that Hugh Padgham brought to the album. Rutherford later remarked that when they came to work on the remasters around 2007, as soon as they reached the albums produced by Padgham, they sounded 'bloody good'. Listening to this thirty or so years later there is much about the song that dates it, none more so than the keyboard patches used, but at the time this was as close to a perfectly formed, radio-friendly pop ballad as it gets.

'Anything She Does' 4:06 (Banks, Collins, Rutherford)

This song begins with more keyboard brass and lyrics – again from Banks – who says the song was inspired by the scantily clad pictures of women they might pin up on the studio walls. It tells of a man who is in love with a porn star. Even though the song was never released as a single, a video was produced for it that featured British comedian Benny Hill in his 'Fred Scuttle' guise, as the band's incompetent security guard. It was never played live, as Banks says it was too difficult to perform, but the video was shown on the screen at the start of the *Invisible Touch* tour before the band took to the stage.

In complete contrast to 'In Too Deep', 'Anything She Does' is the rockiest number on Invisible Touch. The song has strong hints of the Police about it, both from the drumming – very much the style of Stewart Copeland – and the vocal delivery, especially the 'no no never' refrain used at the end of the song, which sounds a lot like Sting.

'Domino' 10:42 (Banks, Collins, Rutherford)

As explained so charmingly by Collins during gigs, the 'Domino Principle' describes how the actions of one person or group can ripple across a huge distance and influence others – not dissimilar to the Butterfly Effect. This song would feature on all the band's subsequent tours, including *Calling All Stations*. It is the one track from the album that was a departure from the short, commercial pop song format, harkening back to the band's earlier albums. As a taster for new fans to the longer-form version of the band, it will hopefully have encouraged many to check out Genesis' earlier work. 'Part One: In the Glow of the Night' is set in a Beirut hotel room just after bombs start to fall. Banks wrote the lyrics based on the 1982 Lebanon War, revolving around the idea that a guy had lost his woman to the violence and is saying 'look what you've done' to the person who pressed the button on the conflict. 'Part Two: The Last Domino' developed out of a jam session and was called 'Hawkwind' as it reminded the band of the group of the same name. The 'Domino' jam sessions also spawned the basic riff that would become 'Invisible Touch'. It is more frantic than the first part of the song, in order to portray the feeling of helplessness that one feels that there is nothing you can do when 'you're next in line'.

The number starts moodily, with a marimba-style rhythm and breathy synthesiser riff supporting the main melody before the Simmons electronic drums kick in, dominating the arrangement. The hauntingly beautiful and reflective 'In silence and darkness' section perfectly prepares us for the rockier 'blood on the windows' part. Not content to play the rockier theme out till the end, we are treated to further changes in tempo and mood, with the slow keyboard solo at 6:20 creating one of my favourite moments on the album.

The ending is a disappointing fade out, which was improved on when played live with a dramatic chord change to end the piece. I've often wondered what impression a track such as 'Domino' left on a listener who bought the album based on liking 'In Too Deep' for example. Given how popular the song clearly was live, it must have been a positive experience for many.

'Throwing It All Away' 3:51 (Banks, Collins, Rutherford)

This is one of the simplest songs on the album, both in terms of melody and lyric, but is one of the most effective. It is the poignant story of a break up from one side of the relationship. The lyrics are cutting, but at the same time quite matter of fact, as if they are the reflective, rationalised thoughts recalled some time later, rather than in the heat of the break-up. 'We cannot live together. We cannot live apart' highlights the struggle of a love-hate relationship. The title of the song and its chorus propose that everything – including all the good left in the relationship – is being thrown away because of the bad parts in it. There is still clearly love for the other person in lines like 'Who'll light up the darkness? Who will hold your hand? Who will find the answers, when you don't understand?' Collins has confirmed, not surprisingly, that this was about his divorce, and given that the break up took place over seven years earlier, the distance and philosophical nature of the lyrics make sense.

Rutherford's guitar brings obvious comparisons with 'Follow You. Follow Me', and while the song does have a similar feel, this is a far more accomplished composition. The arrangement is straight forward but still exhibits a high degree of polish. It was first released as a single in the US on 8 August 1986, with an edit of 'Do the Neurotic' as the B-side, reaching number four, and released much later in the UK on 8 June 1987 with 'I'd Rather Be You' as the B-side, reaching number 22 in the charts.

'The Brazilian' 4:49 (Banks, Collins, Rutherford)

This is the only instrumental on the album and one of my favourite tracks from it, especially when the piece breaks into the middle solo section, rounding off with one of Rutherford's best guitar solos. The track won out over 'Do The Neurotic', the other instrumental recorded at the time, for inclusion on the album. An idea inspired by Banks, it was featured on the movie *When The Wind Blows*, whose soundtrack was produced by Roger Waters. The track was nominated for a Grammy in 1987 under the category 'Best Pop Instrumental Performance (Orchestra, Group or Soloist)' losing out to the 'Top Gun Anthem' from Harold Faltermeyer and Steve Stevens.

Related Tracks
'Feeding the Fire' 5:49 (Banks, Collins, Rutherford)

The verse of this song has a great vocal from Collins, spoilt somewhat by the addition of synthesiser brass. After the reaction to 'No Reply At All,' you can understand the band not wanting to bring in the Phenix Horns again, but it would have been better to have avoided a synthetic brass section. It has something of a lame chorus, and overall feels weak enough to have been left off the album correctly. It was released as the B-side to 'Land of Confusion', in November 1986.

'I'd Rather Be You' 3:57 (Banks, Collins, Rutherford)

This is a bouncy, easy-going Motown-style song – and feels inspired by many of the songs Collins had been recording in his solo career, especially for the movie soundtrack to *Buster*. Again, it was the correct choice to leave it as a B-side – in this case to 'Throwing It All Away' – in July 1987.

'Do the Neurotic' 7:07 (Banks, Collins, Rutherford)

This is an instrumental that vied with 'The Brazilian' for inclusion on the album, and that may not have been an easy choice. The start of the piece is something of a mish-mash of sounds, with Collins playing what sounds like pots, pans and other kitchen utensils, before a drum and guitar riff very similar to The Police plays out. There is some great guitar work by Rutherford here, but it goes on way too long. Had they cut the rather odd introduction and shortened the piece overall, this could well have been a better choice than 'The Brazilian' for the instrumental track. It was released as the B-side to 'In Too Deep', in August 1986.

We Can't Dance (1991)

Personnel:
Tony Banks: keyboards
Phil Collins: drums, percussion, vocals, drum machines
Mike Rutherford: guitars, bass guitar
Recorded at The Farm, Surrey between March and September 1991
Producer: Genesis and Nick Davis
Sleeve design: Icon Photography with illustrations by Felicity Roma Bowers
Released: October 28, 1991
Label: Virgin in the UK and Atlantic in the US
Highest Chart places: UK: 1, US: 4. Achieved quadruple platinum in the US
(4,000,000), five times platinum in the UK (1,500,000), five times platinum in
Germany (1,000,000), double platinum in France (200,000) and platinum in
Australia (70,000)
Running time: 71:30

After a gap of five years, given the major success of *Invisible Touch*, a follow up
was always going to be tricky. *We Can't Dance* didn't sell as well in the US as
Invisible Touch but still achieved four platinum awards, which were the same
number as *Genesis* had achieved. It reached number one in the UK, making it
five in a row for the band's studio recordings, topping many other European
charts and achieving platinum in multiple countries worldwide. For me, *We
Can't Dance* was a return to form, with some very strong tracks like 'No Son
of mine', 'Driving the Last Spike' and, of course, the highlight, 'Fading Lights'.
The band's, 60-date world tour in 1992 included six nights at Earls Court in
London and a headline spot at the Knebworth festival, which was undoubtedly
the peak for Genesis in terms of commercial success and popularity as a live
act. My journey to Knebworth with friends John and Graeme are memories
to be treasured, and the gig was fantastic. John and I almost got to the front,
although the journey back to Scotland was less memorable. The presence of
support acts like current chart successes The Saw Doctors and Lisa Stansfield
on the same bill illustrated how much Genesis' fan base had changed. The
band were now a fully-fledged pop/rock group, with a big enough draw to
receive sponsorship from Volkswagen for their world tour. The band continued
to be a major force in the German charts where *We Can't Dance* was at number
one for an astonishing 24 weeks, selling five million copies. This success would
be reflected later in the selection of locations for the European leg of the
reunion tour in 2007, with a strong emphasis on German venues.

During the break since the *Invisible Touch* tour, the band had been busy
with several side projects. Collins had started working on his train set, starred
in the movie *Buster*, playing the great train robber Buster Edwards, and had
released *But Seriously* in 1989 along with a world tour in support of that
album. Rutherford had released *Living Years* with Mike and the Mechanics
in 1988, for which he won an Ivor Novello award for the title track, along

with co-writer B. A. Robertson. That single reached number one in the US and number two in the UK. The follow-up, Word of Mouth had just been released when the band started recording *We Can't Dance*. Banks had released an album under the name Bankstatement in 1989, and another solo album, Still, in 1991.

Previous releases had all been in the region of 45 to 47 minutes, however due to the advent of CD, the fashion for bonus tracks and the apparent need to fill up all the available media, *We Can't Dance* came in at over 71 minutes long, with only two tracks recorded at the time not making the released album. As a result, several tracks could have been omitted without being missed, and shortening it may well have resulted in a stronger album. 'Tell Me Why', 'Living Forever' and 'Way Of The World' would all have been strong candidates for exclusion, not to mention with the possible addition of the excellent 'On The Shoreline', a strong track released as a B-Side to 'I Can't Dance'.

It was another project written as a trio at the Farm, although this time they returned to the technique of all three of them bringing ideas to the writing session, rather than starting from scratch as they had done for the last couple of releases. Nick Davis was brought in to help with production, having worked with Banks on *Still* earlier the same year. Five singles were released, with 'I Can't Dance' being the most successful, peaking at number seven in both the UK and US, while 'On The Shoreline' and 'Hearts On Fire' were recorded in the same sessions and were used as B-sides. The cover design was by UK photographer and artist David Scheinmann of Icon photography. Icon was a new company created by Andrew Ellis who had worked as a designer for Island and A&M records as well as Hipgnosis with Scheinmann also designing Gabriel's *Us* cover. The illustrations were by Felicity Roma Bowers from an image called Fragment.

'No Son of Mine' 6:42 (Banks, Collins, Rutherford)
After the 2007 *Turn It On Again: The Tour*, Collins referred to this and 'Los Endos' as the best Genesis songs, although his opinion, it must be said, was mainly based on how happy he was with his drumming on them. The lyrics tell of an abusive father although, according to Collins, whether it was the Son or the Mother who were being abused was deliberately left ambiguous. The groaning sound used through the verse – which Banks describes as sounding like an 'elephant being sick' – was a guitar sampled on an EMU Emulator, then slowed down for playback. From the opening metronome of the ticking clock, via the elephant with the upset stomach, the song builds brilliantly to the chorus. It was the first single to be released on 21 October 1991 with 'Living Forever' as the B-side and it peaked at number six in the UK and twelve in the US.

'Jesus He Knows Me' 4:18 (Banks, Collins, Rutherford)
This is a song about corrupt televangelists and how they promise the public both worldly success and eternal salvation – in return for their money. At the

time of recording several high-profile televangelists were under investigation by the media, including Robert Tilton who is said to have been pulling in over $80M per year tax-free for his Word of Faith Family Church. Collins provided the lyrics for this one, and the reggae-style interlude is reminiscent of 'Dreadlock Holiday' by 10cc, hinting at how the money is really used – in the Caribbean for sun and cocktails. Released with 'Hearts on Fire' as the B-side, the song reached number twenty in the UK and 23 in the US.

'Driving the Last Spike' 10:10 (Banks, Collins, Rutherford)

The first of the two 'longs' on the album, this song tells the story of the building of the great railways in the 1800s in England when large workforces would leave their families behind to go off to work for long periods, to live and work in harsh conditions. Collins wrote the lyrics after reading the book *The Railway Navies* by Terry Coleman. Traditionally, Banks would tend to write the lyrics for longer songs, but Collins wanted to try writing an extended lyric, so Banks suggested he try this one. The song follows a similar style to 'Domino' and is only about 30 seconds shorter in length. Like 'Domino' it starts quietly, building gradually but with surprises along the way. Rutherford's guitar provides a lovely introduction with a motif that continues through the quieter passages in a subtle, understated fashion. Halfway through, there is superb interplay between guitar and keyboards, continuing under the lyric 'We worked in gangs for all we were worth'. The song slows, to deliver Collins' empathetic lyrics which pinpoint the dangers the workers endured: 'the smoke cleared, the dust it settled. No-one knew how many had died' and then the song powers through to the end. This is the most fulfilling track on the album, and when we experienced it live at Knebworth in 1992, the band played it just as the sun was setting, with the stage smoke drifting on the wind, lit by the fading light. Meanwhile, vintage railway worker images played on all three of the huge 'Jumbotron' screens. It made for an atmosphere that was spine-tingling.

'I Can't Dance' 4:02 (Banks, Collins, Rutherford)

In an interview, Collins discussed how the song actually has nothing to do with 'dancing', as such, but was about male models who looked great, but couldn't string a sentence together and were simply paid to 'just standing here, selling'. It was released as a single on 30 December 1991 with 'On the Shoreline' as the B-side and reached number seven in both the UK and US charts. It was nominated for a Grammy in 1993 in the category 'Best pop performance by a duo or group with vocals' but lost out to Celine Dion and Peabo Bryson with 'Beauty and the Beast'. The 'walk' in the video came from Collins' time at stage school where he noticed that the worst dancers would always lead with the hand and leading foot on the same side.

It is a quirky song, in total contrast to the previous track, and was much more commercially successful than most expected. It demonstrates how popular they were at this time, personifying the cheeky, mischievous side of the group, a feature of most of their studio albums. While I'm no huge fan of the humorous side of the band, I would still far rather listen to this than 'Illegal Alien' or 'Who Dunnit?'. It is another song based around a guitar riff with the addition, in this case, of a 'pots and pans' rhythm section mostly comprising triggered keyboard samples. It is by far the simplest song on the album and is probably the most basic arrangement ever from Genesis, with the same riff on guitar and electric piano carrying through the entire song, verse and chorus, except for the short break for the 'and checking everything is in place, you never know who's looking on' lyric. Sometimes simplicity, a catchy rhythm, a strong hook line and a quirky video works, given the number seven slot on both sides of the Atlantic, making this song the most successful of the six singles released from *We Can't Dance*.

'Never a Time' 3:52 (Banks, Collins, Rutherford)
This is a slightly more upbeat ballad than 'Hold On My Heart', but it is in a similar vein with some nice understated rhythm and lead guitar work from Rutherford. It was the fifth single to be released in the US in November 1992 with live versions of 'Dreaming While You Sleep', 'Turn It On Again' and 'Tonight, Tonight, Tonight' as B-sides, and reaching number 21 in the main chart and number four in the Adult Contemporary chart.

'Dreaming While You Sleep' 7:17 (Banks, Collins, Rutherford)
This track has another dark lyric, hidden in a seemingly innocuous song. Someone driving tired at night hits a woman who steps into the street and fails to stop. She is left in a coma, and he is then haunted by the memory of her 'I will never be free all my life...till the day that you open your eyes. Please open your eyes'. A marimba and drum machine loop play throughout the song, which is lifted during the chorus by a huge, reverberated drum sound – probably the highlight of the song.

'Tell Me Why' 5:00 (Banks, Collins, Rutherford)
This is a rather bouncy, 60's style song contrasting with the lyrics about trying to understand the injustice in the world, of people dying, sleeping rough and asking why God doesn't seem to be listening, in a return to the theme explored in Collins' solo composition 'Another Day In Paradise'. Musically it doesn't explore anything new and sounds rather too familiar with a very basic drum beat and metronomic, somewhat plodding keyboard chords. This is one of several tracks that led to the excessive length of the album that could easily have been removed and wouldn't really have been missed. The track was released as a single on 8 February 1993 with a live version of 'Invisible Touch' as the B-side. It reached number 40 in the UK and failed to chart in the US.

'Living Forever' 5:42 (Banks, Collins, Rutherford)

Banks' lyrics discuss the confusion created by the constant bombardment of health information in the media telling you what you should do to remain healthy, often contradicting previous advice on the topic. When faced with this shifting body of advice, the song's character decides 'I think I'll change my life today. Gone are the times of taking care. And I don't need a reason why'. After a brief, promising introduction, both the verse and chorus are dull and lack inspiration. Only when the 'I know we don't need you' part comes in at 1:53 does the song start to get interesting, but only briefly as it returns to another bland verse and chorus. Almost as an afterthought, the best part of the song is the instrumental section in the second half where Banks solos over Rutherford's funky guitar, ending with a reprise of the introduction. This excellent end section could have worked so much more had it been combined with a more interesting song, so goes down as an opportunity missed.

'Hold on My Heart' 4:39 (Banks, Collins, Rutherford)

You would be forgiven for thinking this was a Collins-originated song, so like his solo material is this ballad, but Banks brought this idea to the writing sessions. It is a mundane, quiet ballad that, if I'm honest, created the perfect opportunity to take a restroom break or go to the bar during the live sets. It's that dull. The lyrics are about someone hesitant to give their love again after being hurt before. The song was, nonetheless, released as a single on 6 April 1992 with 'Way of the World' as the B-side, it reached number sixteen in the UK, number twelve in the US and an astonishing number one in Canada.

'Way of the World' 5:40 (Banks, Collins, Rutherford)

This song is an instant foot-tapper from the opening notes of the introduction, then pares back the arrangement to a simple verse, lifted by the brighter chorus using the same chords as the introduction. Again, the song feels like it might have been developed better, but gets stuck in a simple drum pattern. However, the real star here is the lyric, about the people-made issues that blight the world and the shrug many countries and politicians give when challenged about it, 'There's right, and there's wrong. There's weak, and there's strong. It's just the way of the world. And that's how it's meant to be'.

'Since I Lost You' 4:11 (Banks, Collins, Rutherford)

This is a sad tale of loss, written by Collins after the tragic death of Eric Clapton's four-year-old son Connor. Collins and Clapton had been friends most of their lives, with Collins also producing, and playing on Clapton's *August* and *Behind The Sun*. Unfortunately, it is one of those songs that is easily forgotten despite the huge amount of emotion Collins gives the lyrics. It does sound somewhat out of place on the album and might have been better suited to a Collins solo record, but is probably featured here as the album was recorded in the middle of two of Collins' solo releases. *...But Seriously* had been released two years earlier, and *Both Sides* was another two years away. Given that the tragedy happened in March 1991, this was probably the only medium Collins had to pay the tribute he wanted to. He asked Clapton for his approval before including the song on the album.

'Fading Lights' 10:15 (Banks, Collins, Rutherford)

Banks brought the band this song about the end of something – perhaps a relationship, a career, a life or maybe even, in this case, a band. Perhaps he could sense the end and that this could well be the last song on the last album from Genesis. As it transpired, it was the last song with Phil Collins, but not the last from Genesis itself. When performed live, the song was extended to eleven minutes with only Banks, Collins and Rutherford on stage playing to the drum loop backing, Stuermer and Thompson having vacated the stage. Collins would then play live drums during the middle section, with Rutherford playing a longer – and better – solo than in the studio before Collins returned to the front of the stage to sing the closing section. The sound from just the three studio band members was stunning, creating some spine-tingling moments live – both at Knebworth and no doubt on the rest of the tour.

The track contains another electronic rhythm loop from Collins, with a gorgeous Banks chord progression and single note bass pedal drone and a plaintive Collins vocal. It is almost two minutes into the song before there is a change in the bass note, lifting us into the chorus with the 'These are the days of our lives' lyric. The song builds further in the middle section with guitar, drums and keyboard stabs and Banks' wonderful multi-part keyboard solo, so reminiscent of some of the older songs, before moving into shades of 'Mama'. It is certainly my favourite solo of his from the later Genesis albums. Collins returns with his sad, lamenting vocal to end the song with 'Far away, away, fading distant lights. Leaving us all behind, lost in a changing world. And you know that these are the days of our lives. Remember'. Sections of the song take us back from the latest style of the band through the 1980s and into earlier eras with the extended solos, almost as if it were a summary of the band's entire career. If there hadn't ever been another album, this track and the superb live versions of it would have been a fitting and a lasting memory of a great band.

Banks admits that he did realise that this could be their last album, saying.

When I wrote the lyric to 'Fading Lights' – another of my 'terminal' songs – I had the idea of ending the song with the word 'remember', and it is very poignant in that context, because it marked the end of a large part of our career.

Related Tracks
'On the Shoreline' 4:47 (Banks, Collins, Rutherford)

I like this track, a lot. The introduction borrows something from 'No Son of Mine' with the sampled, groaning guitar and simple drum beat. It has a plain, two-chord verse that is refreshingly simple while the bridge at 2:39 that begins, 'Can you take me there' is one of catchiest moments of pop music from Genesis that didn't make it onto an album. It was released as the B-side to 'I Can't Dance' in December 1991.

'Hearts on Fire' 5:14 (Banks, Collins, Rutherford)
This track is inspired by the electronic hits of the day (think Harold Faltermeyer) with a fat, synthesised bass. However, there's nothing else that was memorable about the song, and it was certainly the correct choice to leave this out as it is weaker than the other tracks that were included on the final album. It was released as the B-side to 'Jesus He Knows Me' in July 1992.

Calling All Stations (1997)

Personnel:
Ray Wilson: lead vocals
Tony Banks: keyboards, acoustic guitar, backing vocals
Mike Rutherford: guitars, bass, backing vocals
Nir Zidkyahu: drums on 'Calling All Stations', 'Congo', 'Shipwrecked', 'Alien
Afternoon' (second half), 'Not About Us', 'The Dividing Line', 'Uncertain Weather',
'There Must Be Some Other Way', and 'One Man's Fool', percussion
Nick D'Virgilio: drums on 'Alien Afternoon' (first half), 'If That's What You Need',
'Uncertain Weather', and 'Small Talk', percussion
Recorded at the Farm, Surrey between January and June 1997
Producer: Nick Davis, Tony Banks and Mike Rutherford
Sleeve design: Wherefore Art?
Released: 2 September 1997
Label: Virgin (UK) and Atlantic (US)
Highest Chart places: UK: 2, US: 54. Achieved gold status in the UK (100,000),
Germany (100,000) and France (50,000)
Running time: 67:42

It was hard to believe the last studio album from Genesis was released
over twenty years ago. After a six-year gap, *Calling All Stations* was to be
the fifteenth and last Genesis studio album to date and having lost yet
another member of the band, which would seem a tad careless, it may have
been poignant to have called the album '… And Then There Were Two …'.
Collins decided to leave the band in March 1996 as he was by then living in
Switzerland and wanted to spend more time with his children. Genesis might
have been expected to be all over without Collins, but Rutherford and Banks
ploughed on via a very lengthy auditioning process which culminated in both
Ray Wilson of Stiltskin and David Longdon, now of the hugely successful
progressive rock band Big Big Train, being taken through rehearsals for the
new album over a period of six months. Wilson was eventually chosen as the
new voice of Genesis. His Scottish band Stiltskin had topped the UK charts in
1994 with their post-grunge single 'Inside' which had originally been written
for an advert for Levi's on British TV. Banks and Rutherford had heard the
Stiltskin album *The Mind's Eye* and could hear some of the qualities of Peter
Gabriel in Wilson's voice. Indeed, Stiltskin had recently split up when Wilson
received a call from Tony Smith asking if he would like to audition to replace
Collins. He says that it was a big decision. He could either sing with one of the
biggest bands in the world or carry on with his 'small career'. With hindsight,
he now says that a big part of him wishes he had carried on with that previous
career.

Having written as a trio for so long, the writing dynamic changed significantly
with the album. While Rutherford felt that Wilson did a very good job,
the chemistry of the 'third person' changed significantly, and Collins was

impossible to replace. His role was often to provide some balance between Banks and Rutherford to allow the band dynamic to work and Collins sums things up well when he says much of the bands material 'washed over him'. He adds that between the three of them, they had the best of all worlds as his own style of writing was 'pretty immediate', Banks' style was rather: 'you may not know it at the moment, but you'll probably be singing this to yourself in a couple of weeks' time' and Rutherford's was somewhere in the middle.

If comparisons can be drawn between the band's solo releases and later albums like *Genesis* and *Invisible Touch*, then this album can perhaps be compared stylistically to an album by Mike and the Mechanics, Rutherford's 'other' band project, still recording and touring today. There are many more songs in a 'standard' song format than on most Genesis albums, which means that too often the songs fall into repetitive, predictable patterns with many similar-sounding arrangements that don't develop as fully as they should. The album may well have benefited from trimming its 67-minute length to highlight the stronger songs. It seems that while Banks had missed out on commercial success as a 'singles' artist, Rutherford was in the middle of a successful chart career with Mike and The Mechanics, so with the writing essentially being down to the two of them, the direction of the album inevitably headed more towards the style of Rutherford than Banks. Overall, if there is one major thing that Collins brings to the table that the album misses, it isn't his drumming, his writing or his singing, but his skill as an arranger. Rutherford has commented on how Collins could take ideas and work them into great songs, knowing how to piece ideas together, often changing the tempo to lift a song to something special. Collins did this with Genesis, his solo albums and several other albums he produced, *Glorious Fool* by John Martyn being an obvious example, and *Calling All Stations* would have benefited from that skill. Even Wilson talks about the lack of any great songs on the album, saying:

All the way through working on the album I was waiting for the song – the 'Mama' or the 'Land Of Confusion' – the song that just jumped out and said. 'I'm your hit, boys'. I never heard it.

Poor sales for the album and very little radio airplay led to slow ticket sales for the US tour that was planned for the end of 1997 which resulted in its initial postponement, and ultimately, it's cancellation. Banks comments that they were booked to play 20,000-seater stadiums but in some cases had only sold 20 or 30 tickets. The European tour took place on in 1998, but the lack of success in the US dampened any enthusiasm, particularly from Rutherford, for the band to continue and no more studio albums have been produced since. Wilson was contracted for a second album and quite rightly feels that Rutherford's decision not to continue could have been better communicated. The end was, in his words 'death by silence', waiting a year after the tour was completed to be told that the band was over. Banks has said that he would have liked to have worked with Wilson again, even bringing Nir Zidkyahu on drums and Anthony Drennan (the guitarist from the tour) into the studio to develop another album. It was not to happen, as Rutherford simply didn't want to work at developing a new direction for Genesis. He was still enjoying some success through albums and tours with Mike and The Mechanics and points out that in order to develop a new direction, it would have taken two or three albums and long tours for each to get there, and by that time he had run out of energy and enthusiasm for the band. Listening to the album now, it is possible to detect the lack of passion and commitment during the project's development. In a lot of ways, this was the *Abacab* for the fans of the *Invisible Touch* era of the band – another necessary step in the change of direction towards a different band. Who can know what we might have heard had they pushed through the growing pains and allowed another era to develop? Anthony Drennan would go on to feature on the last two Mike and The Mechanics albums, *The Road* in 2011 and *Let Me Fly* in 2017.

This was to be the first Genesis studio album since *...and then there were three...* in 1978 not to reach number one in the UK album charts, ending a run of five number one studio albums in a row. It did, however, reach number two in the UK – a good result by any measure. However, It was, also the first since Selling England By The Pound not to reach the US top 50. To put *Calling All Stations* in perspective, however, in purely commercial terms, it ranks the ninth bestselling studio album out of all fifteen. It outsold every Gabriel era album except *The Lamb Lies Down On Broadway* and sold more than *Seconds Out* and *Wind & Wuthering* from the Collins era. Released at a time where peer to peer music file sharing was on the rise leading to a drop in album sales, accurate comparisons are hard to make, but there might have been something to build on.

Three singles were released from the album, none of which entered the Billboard Top 100 charts, with only 'Congo' managing to get to number 25 in the US Mainstream Rock charts. In the UK things were slightly better with 'Congo' reaching number 29, but 'Shipwrecked' and 'Not About Us' only managing 54 and 66 respectively. Even in Germany, one of the major fanbases of the band, 'Congo' only reached number 31 and the other two singles failed to get above number 80. The cover was another designed by Wherefore ART? With photography from Kevin Westernberg and Peter Robathan.

'Calling All Stations' 5:43 (Banks, Rutherford)
We can tell immediately, right from opening bars, that this is once again a different Genesis sound with its heavier, more prominent and more aggressive guitar. Dark keyboard pads reminiscent of 'Mama' fill the soundscape, and when the vocals start, Wilson sounds confident and in control, although the opening lines of the album, 'Can anybody tell me, tell me exactly where I am, I've lost all sense of direction', might well have summed up where Genesis were at this point in their career. Rutherford adds a decent guitar solo to the

track, having grown in confidence over the twenty years since Hackett had left. Overall, the song is a dark, dramatic, almost traditional-style Genesis song and a great way to open the album, remaining Wilson's favourite.

'Congo' 4:51 (Banks, Rutherford)

In May 1997, towards the end of the recording process for *Calling All Stations*, many Rwandan refugees had fled the Angolan conflict into Congo and took part in the Congolese civil war which started on 5 June 1997.

Opening with the African rhythm and tribal chanting of 'Congo' (that was dropped from the single version the song) this is another great, powerful track with big production including a huge distorted keyboard sound in the verse and full widescreen keyboards in the chorus. Wilson's low, gravelly voice menaces in the verse before opening up in the chorus. In order to avoid repetition and maintain attention two short instrumental breaks are used, the first halfway through the track with the 'Into my heart you came' lyric, and another at the end after the somewhat lacklustre solo beginning 'I would never be the one to say you had no reason'. Backed by a lavish and expensive looking video, this was the first and most successful of the three singles from the album, released on 15 September 1997 with 'Papa He Said' and 'Banjo Man' as B-sides, reaching number 29 in the UK charts. It was the only single from the album to break into the UK top 40.

'Shipwrecked' 4:23 (Banks, Rutherford)

On Wilson's first day in the studio, he reports that while Banks read a newspaper, Rutherford enthused over a new song he had called 'Shipwrecked', insisting on (badly) singing the chorus. Wilson tried to remain professional and not knowing where to look, saw Banks' newspaper shaking. He eventually dropped his paper and burst out laughing. It helped break the ice and also demonstrated that the often stern-faced Banks does have a sense of humour after all.

The song is a simple tale of the breakup of a relationship, 'Why do you say you want to be with me, but the next day you say you don't' is the key line, with 'I can't believe what you said to me' the repeated in the chorus. It is very much a Rutherford song and could have as easily sat on a Mike and The Mechanics album. However, it is certainly one of the stand out tracks and deserved its release as a single in the UK on 1 December 1997 with 'Phret' and '7/8' as B-sides, but, disappointingly, only reached number 54 in the UK charts.

'Alien Afternoon' 7:51 (Banks, Rutherford)

This song has a long keyboard intro that promises much, but it is spoilt by a drab verse, and despite a slightly more inspired bridge, a somewhat poor chorus. Lyrically, it repeats the abduction theme of 'Keep It Dark' from *Abacab*. The second half of the song is better than the first, which is more reminiscent of an earlier 'big' Genesis sound with lush keys, bending guitars and prominent drums fills, but ultimately the piece fails to go anywhere much in its (almost) eight minutes.

'Not About Us' 4:38 (Banks, Rutherford, Wilson)

Wilson contributed the words to this song, one of only three that he had a chance to influence, as most of the album was written before he came on board. The song has a simple arrangement, beginning with acoustic guitar before bringing in keys, bass and drums in turn. It's a great start, and the rest is typical of a Banks song and his love of big choruses. The track was released as a single in the UK on 23 February 1998, with 'Anything Now', 'Sign Your Life Away' and 'Run Out Of Time' as B-sides, reached number 66 in the charts.

'If That's What You Need' 5:12 (Banks, Rutherford)

This is one of those slow love ballads that could easily have been on *We Can't Dance*, especially with Banks' now-familiar keyboard sounds and chords. Despite the decent chorus, middle eight and a short string interlude, the song feels rather like 'songwriting by numbers' and doesn't go anywhere until it fades out over the vocal. The track is a prime example of how it didn't always work out when the band tried to write short, simpler songs.

'The Dividing Line' 7:45 (Banks, Rutherford)

This is one of the better tracks on the album, with a more open feel to it, more akin to some of the band's older songs which they developed through jam sessions. The opening section retains the feel of such a jam and Zidkyahu's drumming is spectacular throughout, having been told to 'hit whatever you like'. Wilson's voice is also in top form here, singing rather dark lyrics about the shadier side of any city across a dividing line where 'the streetlights stop. The colours start to change'. It also has a strong instrumental section, and the song actually ends rather than simply fading out, which is a refreshing change.

'Uncertain Weather' 5:29 (Banks, Rutherford)

'Uncertain Weather' has another lush keyboard arrangement, with a 'Follow You, Follow me' style muted guitar rhythm, and another big chorus complete with some great chord work from Banks. That said, the melody doesn't really fit the arrangement, which is slightly clumsy in places, and of all the songs on the album, this one would have best suited Collins' voice. The lyrics are rather cliched with the references to a faded photograph and footsteps fading in the sand. However already, seven tracks in, we are starting to hear a repetition of song styles and the desire to fill up the CD seems to have been more important than the need to present a good selection of songs across a variety of styles.

'Small Talk' 5:02 (Banks, Rutherford, Wilson)

This track provides a welcomed break from the melancholic tone of many of the other songs, but the relief is short-lived as the repetitive title descends into a forced caricature of other songs of the period. The 'don't talk back to me' and 'small talk' sections sound like a Gabriel solo track, 'Big Time' for example, and Wilson's vocal style has many Gabriel like qualities. The chorus is one of the better ones on the album, and overall the song is both catchy and annoying in equal quantities.

'There Must Be Some Other Way' 7:54 (Banks, Rutherford, Wilson)

It is back to the melancholy once again. While I love it that Banks was filling the arrangement with lots of keyboards, by this point on the album the tone is becoming far too repetitive and there's definitely an impression that you've heard this on the album already. The lift for the chorus is a little too predictable, but Wilson delivers a great vocal performance on the track, showing off the gravelly, rockier side to his voice. The second half of the track allows Banks to give us a good, if familiar, solo before the song slows with pizzicato strings, but then returns for another verse and chorus. Structurally, it may have worked better to have used the solo section to provide a dramatic end, rather than return to a verse, chorus and yet another fade out.

'One Man's Fool' 8:58 (Banks, Rutherford)

While this is the longest song on the album, once again there's a feeling of deja vu here. It takes far too much of its nine minutes to get going before a short solo and guitar section followed by a key change and a somewhat more interesting instrumental break. The section that follows is more driving – one of the most impressive of the album, boosted by an upbeat chorus: 'One man's joy makes another man weep. Nothing you can do is ever gonna change it. One man's saint is another man's fool. One man's hot is another man's cool'. It makes the listener wonder if the band were pre-empting the reaction to the album, suggesting that not everyone would like the music and that they couldn't please everyone. Once again, there is a fade out during the final vocal – a common feature of the album. That said, at least the album ends on something of a high.

Related Tracks:

A staggering eight additional tracks were recorded in the same sessions as *Calling All Stations*, totalling over 40 minutes of material, enough for an old-fashioned vinyl release. All but one of the eight were released on the various multiple-track CD singles that came out.

'Papa He Said' 4:09 (Banks, Rutherford)

This is a simple song that tries to rekindle the hits of *Invisible Touch*, and *We*

Can't Dance but sounds so familiar that this probably led to its exclusion. It was released as a B-side to 'Congo' in the UK in September 1997.

'The Banjo Man' 4:22 (Banks, Rutherford, Wilson)
The 'novelty banjo' sound on this song – a poor choice – gives the name to this track, the best part of which is Wilson's vocal delivery, which sounds rather like Sting from The Police. It was released in the UK as a B-side to 'Congo' in September 1997.

'Phret' 4:05 (Banks, Rutherford)
Unusually for a Genesis album, there were no all-instrumental tracks on *Calling All Stations*, probably due to the presence of Wilson, who, unlike Collins, could contribute little to any instrumentals. More likely this was a backing track for a song that was never completed as it has a simple melody line played through the probable verse, while the probable chorus features fretless bass, which probably contributed to the title of the track. It was released as the B-side to 'Shipwrecked' in December 1997.

'7/8' 5:13 (Banks, Rutherford)
The other instrumental left off of *Calling All Stations* is stronger than 'Phret' but gives us little to cheer about until about 1:20 in, when a stronger theme emerges that grabs the listener. Most likely still a working title based on the time signature, this guitar-driven piece, as with 'Phret', sounds more like a song that hadn't received any lyrics than a true instrumental, given the strong melody lines carried through what would have been the verse and chorus. Indeed, it might have made a strong song. It was released in the UK as a B-side to 'Shipwrecked' in December 1997. Incidentally, if you google 'Genesis 7/8', you are more likely to get the story of Noah and his ark than information on this particular song.

'Anything Now' 7:03 (Banks, Rutherford)
A strong start to this song instantly makes you wonder why it wasn't included on the main release. It is the longest of the extra tracks, but this is mainly due to the last few minutes of pointless piano tinkling from Banks' and a short solo. It has a good, catchy chorus and shows how much of the 80's sound was still retained by Rutherford and Banks after Collins' departure. It was released in the UK as a B-side to 'Not About Us' in February 1998.

'Sign Your Life Away' 4:45 (Banks, Rutherford)
This is another, heavier, guitar-based song, with an overly simple, single-chord verse which sounds rather too much like The Police. It's good, though, and had it been matched up with a better verse, it would probably have made it onto *Calling All Stations*. In the UK, it was released as a B-side to 'Not About Us' in February 1998.

'Run Out of Time' 6:36 (Banks, Rutherford)

The introduction to this song sounds very like the opening part of 'I Can't Dance' but with a sax solo played on synth, something that really should never appear on any song, ever. After all, it's not as if they couldn't have afforded a session player at this point in their career. The song is dominated by a thickly layered, cinematic keyboard texture with lots of guitar soloing throughout the track and shows another side to Wilson's voice that is markedly different in the style and range used on the tracks that made the album. Reminiscent of the style of Mike and the Mechanics, it was released in the UK as the B-side to 'Not About Us' in February 1998.

'Nowhere Else to Turn' 4:35 (Banks, Rutherford, Wilson)

This was the only additional track never to see a release at the time, but for no good reason other than it sounds like Mike and The Mechanics once again. It's a good song, both the verse and the chorus work nicely, and there is little doubt that had Wilson been invited as a guest vocalist by Rutherford for his 'other band', his voice would have worked very well, and he wouldn't have been subjected to the level of scrutiny he received as part of Genesis.

Live Albums
Genesis Live (1973)
Personnel:
Peter Gabriel: lead vocals, flute, tambourine, bass drum
Tony Banks: Hammond Organ, Mellotron, Hohner Pianet, 12-string guitar, backing vocals
Steve Hackett: lead guitar
Mike Rutherford: bass guitar, Dewtron 'Mister Bassman' bass pedal synthesiser, 12-string guitar, backing vocals
Phil Collins: drums, percussion, backing vocals
Recorded at De Montfort Hall, Leicester on 25 February 1973, except 'Return of the Giant Hogweed' which was recorded the previous night at the Free Trade Hall in Manchester.
Producer: John Burns and Genesis
Sleeve design: Chris Peyton. Front photo by Bob Gruen
Released: 3 August 1973
Label: Charisma
Highest Chart places: UK:9, US:105
Running time: 46:44

Genesis Live was originally recorded for an American radio show, , but was never broadcast. Charisma wanted to release the tapes, but the band didn't agree initially, unable to see the benefit of a non-studio release at a time when new material was already available. Upon their agreement, it was released between *Foxtrot* and *Selling England by the Pound* but did not include 'Supper's Ready' which was their favourite – and best – live piece at the time, as the band didn't want to have such a long piece on two consecutive releases. 'Supper's Ready' had been recorded at the time, and the cover photograph of the album was taken from a live performance of the track with Gabriel in his Magog costume. This version of the piece would be released later as part of the 1998 compilation *Genesis Archive 1967-75*, and a rare two-disc promo version of the album was released which did have 'Supper's Ready' included.

The band were not entirely happy with their sound on record and struggled to get the big live sound they had developed onto a studio album. While the audio quality here isn't fantastic, it does give a much fuller sound to the songs and the energy they had as a live band really comes across well, making the songs superior to their studio versions in many ways.

The back cover features a short story written by Gabriel, telling of a woman who starts to strip on an underground train. As she removes her clothes, she continues with her skin and eventually all that is left is a tube of light. The imagination shown in this piece attracted the attention of William Friedkin the director of *The Exorcist*, leading to an offer of work for Gabriel during the writing of *The Lamb Lies Down On Broadway* the following year. The sleeve design was by Chris Peyton using a photograph by Bob Gruen.

The album opens with 'Watcher of the Skies' as indeed did the set. Those big Mellotron chords and the white backdrop set against lots of dry ice made for an impressive start to the show. It continues with 'Get 'em Out by Friday', featuring several changes in tempo with Rutherford running up and down the neck of his bass, and Banks playing multiple parts on organ and Mellotron. Collins puts in an energetic performance, but there is also finesse in the quieter parts. We hear Hackett's instantly recognisable guitar sound and Gabriel using multiple vocal styles, but most importantly, we can truly hear how tight and accomplished Genesis were as a band at this stage, after three years of gigging and four studio albums. 'The Return of the Giant Hogweed' is another complex piece, and next is 'The Musical Box', although the spoken introduction from Gabriel was removed from this version. He would tell the tale of Henry and Cynthia's fateful croquet match, and while this piece would feature on many tours for the next 25 years, this is the only full version of this song available on an official live album. The set ends with 'The Knife', which was the biggest, boldest and most upbeat song in the live set at the time, and was used as the set closer at many gigs.

The album was reissued in 2007 to coincide with the Turn It On Again: The Tour and included five additional tracks that were recorded on the tour on 24 February 1975 at the Shrine Auditorium in Los Angeles. The five tracks would later appear with the complete live recording of the album on the Genesis Archive 1967-1975 released in 1998. 'Back in N.Y.C.', 'Fly on a Windshield', 'Broadway Melody of 1974','Anyway' and 'The Chamber of 32 Doors'.

Seconds Out (1977)

Personnel:
Tony Banks: Hammond T. organ, RMI Electra Piano, Mellotron M400, ARP Pro Soloist synthesisers, Epiphone 12-string acoustic guitar, backing vocals
Phil Collins: lead vocals, Premier and Gretsch drums, percussion
Steve Hackett: Gibson Les Paul electric guitar, Hokada 12-string acoustic guitar
Mike Rutherford: Shergold electric 12-string guitar and bass, 8-string bass, Alvarez 12-string acoustic guitar, Moog Taurus bass pedals, backing vocals
Chester Thompson: Pearl Drums and percussion
Bill Bruford: Hayman and Ludwig drums and percussion on 'The Cinema Show.'
Recorded at Palais de Paris in Paris from 11 to 14 June 1977, with 'The Cinema Show' recorded a year earlier on 23 June 1976 at Pavillon de Paris.
Producer: David Hentschel and Genesis
Sleeve design: A&D Design with photos from Armando Gallo, Robert Ellis and Graham Wood.
Released: 21 October 1977
Label: Charisma in the UK and Atlantic in the US.
Highest Chart places: UK:4, US:47. Achieved gold in the UK (100,000).
Running time: 95:31

Seconds Out still stands as one of the greatest live albums ever recorded, and it captures a band in top form playing versions of the music that were often better than those recorded in the studio. The album was recorded over four nights in Paris during June 1977 during the *Wind & Wuthering* tour, with 'Cinema Show' being recorded on the *Trick of the Tail* tour a year earlier. This was the second tour in which Collins took on the multiple roles of drummer, vocalist and frontman. His confidence had grown from the previous tour, and his comfort level really showed as he held the audience for the entire performance. The band were touring with a major show by now, including their '747 lights' – 48 of the same landing lights used on the jumbo jet forming an intensely bright light curtain. Collins felt all the lights, lasers, bells and whistles really enhanced his role as frontman. Given that this was recorded on the *Wind & Wuthering* tour, surprisingly only one song – 'Afterglow' – is included from that album, even though 'Eleventh Earl of Mar', 'One for the Vine' and 'Your Own Special Way' were played throughout the tour, with 'All In A Mouse's Night' also played on the UK dates.

Just a couple of weeks before the release of *Seconds Out*, on 8 October 1977, the official announcement was made that Hackett was leaving the band. Banks joked on the *Genesis: A History* video that 'we just mixed him out of the rest of the album and that was it, really'. Indeed at times, Hackett's guitar does seem inordinately quiet, but it is hard to believe that the rest of the band would be so spiteful to potentially lower the quality of the live album by such a deliberate act. Having found a new freedom and responsibility while recording *Voyage of the Acolyte*, the claustrophobia of the band became even more oppressive for Hackett. Unhappy with some of the song selections on the previous two releases, he recalls numerous meetings and arguments with rest of the band, about whom he said 'they are at best colleagues and, at worst, competitors.' He was told, in effect not to be a naughty boy, just get on with being a part of the group and not to do solo albums, even in his spare time.

Hackett decided to leave and concentrate on *Please Don't Touch*, which was released just two months after *...and then there were three...* He has very fond memories of his time with the band, and learned a lot, but says 'I felt I had to take the risk in order to find out just how good I was on my own'.

There was no apparent drama in Hackett's leaving, and Rutherford says he can't really remember why he did. Collins was heading to the studio to continue mixing Seconds Out and passed Hackett at a taxi rank, but when he stopped to offer him a lift he said 'No, no, it's ok, I'll call you later'. When Collins arrived at the studio, he was told that Hackett had left the band. Collins later heard that Hackett knew that if he had taken the lift from Collins, he was the one person that would have talked him out of leaving the band. However, Banks was disappointed, feeling that he had lost an ally as they both liked the weirder aspects of the band's music.

The sleeve design was by A&D Design with photos from Armando Gallo, a long time Genesis fan and photographer, as well as Robert Ellis and Graham

Wood. The Genesis logo on the cover returned to the angular version seen on *The Lamb Lies Down On Broadway*.

'Squonk' is a cracking way to open a gig, with a huge live sound. The ending was modified with a new chord sequence to finish the song off live as the studio version was faded out. 'The Carpet Crawl' is a modified name for an altered version of this slower song from *The Lamb Lies Down On Broadway*, starting with the second verse. The sequencing of the album was constrained by the length of a side of vinyl and, of course, 'Supper's Ready' took up a full side. This song was never played straight after 'Squonk' as that sequence wouldn't have worked in a live show, though in some sets it was performed second after 'The Eleventh Earl Of Mar'. 'Robbery, Assault and Battery' was a great live song. Something of a comic piece on the album, it came into its own with Collins dressing up and portraying the characters on stage, his acting experience helping with the live performance, although this, of course, is lost on the audio recording with Banks' solos the main highlights of the song. During the tour, the instrumental '...In That Quiet Earth' set the scene perfectly for 'Afterglow', but this was cut from the album, probably due to space restrictions.

The piano introduction for 'Firth Of Fifth' was dropped during this tour with the song starting with the vocal line 'The path is clear', and Gabriel's flute solo was replaced with Banks and Hackett playing in unison. 'I Know What I Like (In Your Wardrobe)' was one of many songs that came into its own in the live set, as it introduced Collins performing a tambourine 'solo' dance, which was admittedly lost on listeners who hadn't seen the shows live. This version includes short snippets of 'Dancing With The Moonlit Knight', 'Stagnation', 'Visions Of Angels', and 'Blood On The Rooftops' spread through the song. If you can't spot them, they are at 5:04, 5:30, 5:59, and 6:30 respectively. 'The Lamb Lies Down On Broadway' was played as the encore along with 'The Musical Box' on the tour, but lacking a real piano, or even the ability to recreate one onstage in 1977, Banks uses a muted pad to play the piano intro and rhythm throughout the song. This led into 'The Musical Box (Closing Section)' which features the end section of the song starting with 'She's a lady.'. Now with full, belting bass pedals from Rutherford, this formed a powerful end to the show and one of the few tracks where we can clearly hear Hackett's great guitar solo. In later tours, this would be used as the intro to 'Afterglow'.

'Supper's Ready' is an updated arrangement of the classic epic played again on this tour, having been reintroduced on the previous *A Trick of the Tail* excursion. Collins handles the complexities of the vocals with ease. He is soulful and introspective in the earlier sections but powers it out at the end and the double drumming on the 'Apocalypse in 9/8' section is spectacular. During the interviews for the remixes, Nick Davis confirmed that the track was pieced together from sections recorded on three of the four nights in Paris.

'The Cinema Show' was recorded during the *A Trick of the Tail* tour with Bill Bruford on drums, who's jazz swing is evident on the track. Phil's plaintive vocal works well on this song, the highlight being the Banks' long solo which is just superb. 'Dance on a Volcano' was played together with 'Los Endos' as the last number before the encore and the double drumming on 'Los Endos' sounds amazing and builds as a fantastic, end-of-set number, with Hackett's wailing guitar a spectacular highlight. If you weren't there, try to imagine the visual spectacle of two drum kits, played in sync, a huge the wall of sound and a massive curtain of white light. It was such a fantastic end to the show and, as they say, 'the crowd went wild'.

Three Sides Live (1982)

Personnel:
Phil Collins: drums, lead vocals
Tony Banks: keyboards, backing vocals
Mike Rutherford: guitar, bass guitar, backing vocals
Steve Hackett: guitar on 'It/Watcher of the Skies'
Daryl Stuermer: guitar, bass
Chester Thompson: drums. percussion
Bill Bruford: drums on 'it/Watcher of the Skies'
Recorded at various locations between 1976 and 1981
Producer: Genesis
Sleeve design: Bill Smith with photographs by Martyn Goddard
Released: 1 June 1982 in the US, 4 June 1982 in the UK
Label: Charisma in the UK and Atlantic in the US
Highest Chart places: UK: 2, US: 10. Achieve gold in the UK (100,000) and US (500,000).
Running time: 92:42

It is a bit of a misnomer that the album should be called *Three Sides Live* in the UK since all four sides of the original vinyl contain live recordings. The original, international edition, however, replaced side four with the three studio tracks from the *3x3* EP which were tracks recorded at the same time as *Abacab*, plus 'Evidence Of Autumn' and 'Open Door' which were B-sides from singles taken from *Duke*. This was mainly down to the fact that the EP format of *3x3* prevented it from being released in the US, as it was not a popular format there. The 1994 remastered international version would replace side four with the live versions from the original UK release, namely 'One For The Vine', 'Fountain Of Salmacis' and 'it/Watcher Of The Skies'.

Much of the content was recorded during the 1981 *Abacab* tour, with additional older recordings from as far back as 1976. A concert film was released, taken at two shows on the tour at the Savoy Theatre and Nassau Veterans Memorial Coliseum in New York on 28 and 29 November 1981 respectively. Of the tracks included, 'Turn It On Again' opens the album, despite not opening the show, the actual opener 'Behind the Lines' being fourth. 'It / Watcher of the Skies' was recorded at one of the greatest music venues in the world, the Apollo Theatre, Glasgow, Scotland on 8 July 1976, and your author was there. 'Duchess' includes a new intro, extended by almost two and a half minutes featuring a modified drum machine part and additional guitar while 'Misunderstanding' receives Collin's jazzy scat-style improvisation treatment at the end. The old song medley, titled 'In The Cage – Medley' is now extended to almost twelve minutes, or seventeen if you include 'Afterglow'. It is dominated by a long – almost eight minute – version 'In The Cage', which is no bad thing at all, followed by short sections of 'The Cinema Show' and 'The Colony Of Slippermen'. The medley plays straight into 'Afterglow', credited as a separate track, and not part of the medley, the energy of the 'Slippermen' solo from Banks serving to replace the role of '... in that Quiet Place' in building the energy prior to the breakdown for 'Aferglow' that makes it so effective. Always a highlight of any Collins era Genesis show, the medley would continue to grow with subsequent tours. Making up for its omission on Seconds Out, 'One For The Vine' is included here from 1981 at the Theatre Royal, Dury Lane, London, and a great version it is too, all eleven minutes four seconds of it.

The album was a big success, peaking at number two in the UK charts, and ten in the US Billboard 100. The sleeve design was by Bill Smith Studios who had provided the design for Duke and Abacab, not that it required much design, a plain white cover with the Genesis logo from Abacab and Three Sides Live written in the same handwriting font.

The Way We Walk
Vol 1: The Shorts (1992)
Personnel:
Phil Collins: lead vocals, drums, percussion
Tony Banks: keyboards, backing vocals
Mike Rutherford: guitar, bass guitar, backing vocals
Daryl Stuermer: bass guitar, guitar, backing vocals
Chester Thompson: percussion, drums
Recorded in various locations in 1986, 1987 and 1992
Producer: Nick David, Robert Colby and Genesis
Sleeve design: Genesis and Icon, with photographs from Lewis Lee and Cesar Vera
Released: 16 November 1992 (9 November)
Label: Virgin in the UK and Atlantic in the US
Highest Chart places: UK:3, US:35. Achieved double Platinum in the UK (600,000) and Gold in the US (500,000).
Running time: 63:05

Vol 2: The Longs (1993)
Personnel: As 'The Way We Walk, Vol 1: The Shorts'
Recorded mainly at Niedersachsenstadion, Hannover, Germany on 10 and 13 July 1992

Producer: Nick Davis, Robert Colby and Genesis
Sleeve design: Genesis and Icon, with photographs from Lewis Lee, Cesar Vera and Max Kohr
Released: 11 January 1993
Label: Virgin in the UK and Atlantic in the US
Highest Chart places: UK:1, US:20. Achieved gold in the UK (100,000) and US (500,000).
Running time: 70:25

Mainly tapping into the 'hits' from the *Invisible Touch* and *We Can't Dance* tours, the first volume of these two live albums reached number three in the UK and number 35 in the US. The sleeve design was a collaboration between the band and Icon, with photographs in the booklet from Lewis Lee and Cesar Vera. The front cover showed the five members of the touring band doing the 'walk' from the 'I Can't Dance' video and the logo created for *We Can't Dance* was used on the cover. Most of the songs were recorded at Niedersachsenstadion in Hannover, Germany in July 1992 with 'Throwing It All Away' from Knebworth Park on the same tour. Strangely, the versions of 'Mama' and 'That's All' were recorded at Wembley Stadium in 1987 with 'In Too Deep' from The Forum in Inglewood, California in 1986. 'No Son Of Mine', in particular, is a brilliant live version of a great song developed and expanded for the 1992 tour. Indeed, only Genesis could classify a seven-minute song as 'short'. 'Throwing It All Away' includes a Collins call and response sections with the crowd which was always great fun. 'I Can't Dance' is a longer, near seven-minute version with an extended intro, though it does include almost 30 seconds of applause. 'Mama' was always a powerful live number and this version is no exception, probably the best version the band recorded while 'Tonight, Tonight, Tonight' is condensed to half the length of the original, sacrificing the instrumental sections, one of the few numbers where the studio version remains superior to the live one.

After its release in 1992, a selection of the longer songs was also released, recorded in Hanover, Germany on the *We Can't Dance* tour. The album went to number one for two weeks in the UK and was the last number one album of any sort to be released by the band, also reaching number twenty in the US charts. The sleeve design was similar to volume one of the live releases, this time using a coloured silhouette version of the photograph of the five live band members doing the 'walk' from *We Can't Dance*. Photography was again by Lewis Lee and Cesar Vera, with Max Kohr also contributing to this album.

The album is most notable for the cleverly-constructed, twenty minute 'Old Medley', which included 'Dance on a Volcano', 'The Lamb Lies Down on Broadway', 'The Musical Box', 'Firth of Fifth' and 'I Know What I Like (In Your Wardrobe)'. As well as the credited tracks in the medley, there are also short parts from 'That's All', 'Illegal Alien', 'Misunderstanding' and 'Follow You, Follow Me'. 'Driving The Last Spike' is another great live adaptation, remaining true to the album version which was already superb, but in the live show now backed by an archive railway construction video of faded still photographs, which of course doesn't come across on the CD version unless you are listening with the tour in your minds eye. A firm favourite is 'Fading Lights' that worked beautifully live with only Banks, Collins and Rutherford on stage recreating the album version perfectly. The 'Drum Duet' – at over six minutes – is something that definitely works better when you can see what is happening. However, without 'Los Endos' afterwards which wasn't played during the 1992 tour – the drum duel led into 'I Can't Dance' – it lacks context and is a bit like listening to a fireworks display, especially considering the 'oohs' from the crowd.

Both CDs are exceptional quality recordings for a live album and capture at least some of the incredible atmosphere that was prevalent during the 1992 tour, especially at the large open-air venues.

Live Over Europe 2007 (2007)

Personnel:
Phil Collins: lead vocals, drums, percussion, stool
Mike Rutherford: 6 and 12-string guitars, bass, bass pedals, backing vocals
Tony Banks: keyboards, backing vocals
Daryl Stuermer: guitars, bass, bass pedals, backing vocals
Chester Thompson: drums, percussion, stool
Recorded at various locations in Europe between June and July 2007
Producer: Nick Davis
Sleeve design: Chris Peyton with photography by Stephanie Pistel
Released: 20 November 2007 (US), 26 November 2007 (UK)
Label: Virgin (UK), Atlantic (US)
Highest Chart places: UK: 51, US: Did not chart. Reached number 1 in Germany.
Achieved silver in the UK (50,000) and gold in Germany (100,00).
Running time: 139:06

A press conference held in the cinema of the Mayfair Hotel, London on 7 November 2006 and hosted by comedian and Genesis fan David Baddiel, was the launch of the marketing for the European leg of *Turn It On Again: The Tour*. The US leg would begin on 7 March 2007. In all, 47 shows were planned, 21 in Europe, with the others in the US and Canada. A 20-minute spot at *Live Eight*, Al Gore's concert at Wembley was also played the same day as the Manchester gig. The tour coincided with the release of 5.1 remixes of the entire back catalogue in the form of multi-disc box sets, and this was perfect publicity. The tour also provided yet another opportunity for a live album and DVD. The *Live Over Europe 2007* album was recorded during the European leg of the tour. Of the twenty-one concerts played in Europe, nine were hosted in Germany, including two nights in Dusseldorf and the only German venue not to sell out was Berlin. The final date of the European tour was a free outdoor concert at the Circus Maximus in Rome, Italy where the band played to an estimated audience of 500,000. The concert was filmed for a DVD release as *When In Rome 2007*.

Almost every song was transposed to a lower key to allow for Collins' reduced range, with only 'Hold On My Heart', 'Follow You, Follow Me' and instrumentals performed as they originally had been. The sleeve design was by Chris Peyton, featuring a distant photograph of the elaborate and innovative stage and back screen used during the tour by Stephanie Pistel.

For this sixth live album from Genesis, this release would be the first to feature every song from the tour setlist, in the order in which were played live, providing the listener with as close to the live experience as possible. The best performances were selected from the European shows to produce the album, from the first night of the tour in Helsinki to the last night at the open air free gig at the Circus Maximus. Much of the setlist was as might have been expected with the inclusion of most of their greatest hits, including the big hits from their number one album *Invisible Touch*: 'Invisible Touch', 'Tonight, Tonight, Tonight', 'Land Of Confusion' and 'Throwing It All Away'. Later hits from *We Can't Dance* were included, 'I Can't Dance' and 'No Son Of Mine'. However, 'Ripples' was a welcome surprise for many having never appeared on any of the previous live albums. The obligatory 'Old Medley' could not possibly be omitted from the set, and this time around the audience was treated to two, the first including parts of 'In The Cage', 'Cinema Show' and 'Duke's Travels' while the other used 'First Of Fifth', 'I Know What I Like (In Your Wardrobe)' and 'Stagnation'. The live song arrangements were pretty much the same as those used on the 1992 tour.

Six Of The Best (1982)
Personnel:
Tony Banks, Phil Collins, Mike Rutherford, Peter Gabriel, Steve Hackett, Daryl Stuermer, Chester Thompson
Recorded at the National Bowl Milton Keynes on 2 October 1982
Running time: 116:48 minutes

Although this is a bootleg, it is notable as, seven years after leaving the band, Gabriel joined the touring line up for a one-off gig to help pay the debts he had accrued as part of the first WOMAD festival. Hackett also joined after a five-year absence but arrived late for the show due to a flight delay from South America and only appeared for the encores. Jonathan King, who had named the band and produced their first album, introduced them. With Gabriel in the middle of a highly successful solo career, the money generated from this show allowed Gabriel's debts to be paid, so that the WOMAD festival could continue. No official recording of the show exists, but several fan recordings have been digitally remastered, some as recently as 2007. Rutherford has said he regretted not filming the show, which took place on his 32nd birthday.

Box Set Releases

Genesis Archive 1967-1975 (1998)

This four CD-set has a superb 80-page booklet and includes a complete recording of *The Lamb Lies Down On Broadway* from 24 February 1975 at the Shrine Auditorium in Los Angeles. Many of Hackett's guitar parts were re-recorded, as he was recovering from an operation on his hand at the time and Gabriel re-recorded many of the vocals as they were often muffled by his costumes or by his lack of breath on stage. It does end up being a bit of a Frankenstein's monster though, as what is heard is a mix of both the original vocal and the new versions recorded 20 years later, switching between the two during the songs. The matchup is decent, but once you know it is there, it's not hard to spot the difference. The last track, 'it' was recorded in the studio as the multi-track ran out of tape before the end of the gig.

A recording of 'Supper's Ready' is included, which was made at the time as the *Genesis Live* release at the De Montfort Hall, Leicester on 25 February. The recording also captures Gabriel's story at the start, about Old Henry writhing naked on the grass, bringing up worms. Henry starts whistling 'Jerusalem' which meant, for the birds, that supper was ready. Several tracks recorded at the Rainbow in London in October 1973 were also included.

Other tracks of note included:

'More Fool Me', an extended live recording of one of Collins' early lead vocal songs, recorded live at the Rainbow, London in October 1973; 'Stagnation' – a live recording made on 10 May 1971 for the BBC show *Sounds of the Seventies* which was a great supporter of progressive rock; 'Twilight Alehouse,' the B-side of 'I Know What I Like (In Your Wardrobe)' released in 1974; 'Happy the Man', a non-album track that was released in 1972 as a single after *Nursery Cryme* with 'Seven Stones' as the B-side; 'Watcher of the Skies' – a short version of the track originally planned as single in 1972 but never released; 'In the Wilderness' an early rough mix without strings, from 1968 and 'Shepherd' recorded on 22 February 1970 for the BBC radio show *Nightride,* with Banks alternating the lead vocals on this with Gabriel. Also from the same show are: 'Pacidy' and 'Let Us Now Make Love'.

'Going Out to Get You' was a demo recorded on 20 August 1969 at Regent Sound Studio, five months after the release of From *Genesis To Revelation.* This must have been the last demo session recorded while the band were still under the management of King and contracted to Decca records and the song was never used on an album. The version of 'Dusk' was also a demo recorded in August 1969 at Regent Sound Studio of a song that would be recorded later on Trespass. This version is slower than the final recording, but it is surprising how close some sections of this early demo are to it, even down to the flute solo. It is also one of the few early demos where Banks is playing organ and not piano. The drum stick clicks used throughout the track like a metronome, become quite annoying long before the six minutes are over.

Various rough mixes of songs from August 1968 were also included, although they failed to appear on the album itself. These are: 'Build Me a Mountain' 'Image Blown Out' and 'One Day'.

Various demos from 1968 are there too: 'Hidden in the World of Dawn', 'Sea Bee', 'The Mystery of the Flannan Isle Lighthouse', 'Hair on the Arms and Legs', 'In the Beginning', "The Magic of Time' (Silver is credited for playing brushes on a biscuit tin) and 'Where the Sour Turns to Sweet', which is a demo of what was originally planned to be the first single. It would eventually be released as the third single from the *From Genesis To Revelation* album although hadn't changed much by the time it was finally released. Also from that era is 'Hey!

There were also three demos from 1967: 'She is Beautiful' was given new lyrics were to become 'The Serpent' on the *From Genesis To Revelation* album. 'Try a Little Sadness' was also included with 'Patricia', an instrumental from the original demo tape recorded in 1967 that was given to Jonathan King. Later, this had lyrics added and became 'In Hiding' on the *From Genesis To Revelation* album.

To promote the album, a press event was arranged at the Heathrow Business Centre on 11 May 1998 with Banks, Collins, Gabriel, Hackett, Phillips, Rutherford and Silver in attendance. The only ex-members of the band who were not at the event were the first drummer, Chris Stewart, who's only recording is the first single 'Silent Sun', drummer John Mayhew who played on *Trespass* and guitarist Mick Barnard who played for a brief period between Phillips and Hackett. the timing of this release is of particular note. The final Genesis show of the *Calling All Stations* tour in Finland had just been played a month earlier, on 5 April. However,those suggesting that it was a reaction to the muted reception for *Calling All Stations* are mistaken, since this release must have been in the planning for some time given the amount of vocal and guitar work required for the live recording of *The Lamb Lies Down On Broadway* and the preparation of such a detailed 80-page booklet.

The package and sleeve design were again by Wherefore ART? The cover picture was by Etienne Bol, with other photographs from Amanda Gallo, Barrie Wentzell, Richard MacPhail, Steve Lovell-Davis Paddy Summerfield, Tony Banks and Mike Rutherford.

Genesis Archive 2: 1976-1992 (2000)

After a gap of over two years since the first archive collection, the Collins-era tracks were released as a three CD set. Given the amount of additional material that had already been released, there wasn't such a large body of material to draw on from this era. Much of the content comes from the two EPs, the many B-sides and the twelve-inch versions of the pop hits, all augmented by several unreleased live recordings. Tracks worthy of special note include a 'work in progress' version of 'Mama' running to 10:43. This is a raw, early version recorded during the development of the song but contains most of the elements of the final recording before the lyrics were written. Collins repeats a few short lines and uses word-like adlib sounds through the song, including what is close to the final melody and meter, providing a great insight into the development of the track.

The Platinum Collection (2004)
This compilation was released in 2004 in the UK and almost a year later in the US. It contains almost four hours of music, representing every album except *From Genesis To Revelation*. The *Platinum Collection* forms a great history of the band with many of the tracks remixed by Nick Davis. The album cover was another design by Chris Peyton and included a set of six images from the back catalogue; *We Can't Dance, Nursery Cryme, A Trick of the Tail, Foxtrot, Duke* and *Invisible Touch*. When *Turn It On Again – The Tour Edition* was released in 2007 this album was withdrawn in the US.

Genesis 1976-1982 (2007)
As part of the renewed interest in the Genesis around the 2007 reunion tour, EMI had Nick Davis and Hugh Padgham work with the band at The Farm on a series of four box sets covering every release since *Trespass* and the all live material they had produced. These were available in limited quantities, aimed at the hardcore Genesis fan who wanted access to everything they could get on the band. The first of these to be released covered the first five albums with Collins on lead vocals. This resulted in a six-CD and six-DVD box set including remixed versions of *A Trick of the Tail, Wind & Wuthering, ...and then there were three..., Duke* and *Abacab*. A DVD accompanied each of the albums with a 5.1 surround sound mix of the album together with interviews, live performances and reproduction tour programs of the period.

One additional CD and DVD pair were included, comprising mainly the tracks from the 3x3 and Spot The Pigeon EPs and B-sides from the singles released during this period, the DVD providing 5.1 surround sound mixes of the same tracks plus a video of 'Paperlate'.

Genesis 1983-1998 (2007)
Following on from the first box set release, the remaining three albums featuring Collins singing, and the final studio album with Ray Wilson were given the same treatment. This time, a five-CD and DVD box set were produced, including remixed versions of *Genesis, Invisible Touch, We Can't Dance* and *Calling All Stations*. Once again a DVD accompanied each of the albums with a 5.1 surround sound mix of the album together with interviews, live performances and reproduced tour programs.

One additional CD and DVD pair was included with extra tracks comprising the B-sides from singles released during this period. The DVD also includes live video selections from the Knebworth concert in 1992 and the two short ten minute sets performed at the Music Managers Forum (MMF) in September 2000 to honour manager Tony Smith, who was presented with the Peter Grant Award for outstanding achievement.

Genesis 1970-1975 (2008)

The third box set, released the year after the reunion tour, focuses on the years when Gabriel was lead vocalist but excludes the first *From Genesis To Revelation* album. It is a seven-CD, six DVD box set including remixed versions of *Trespass, Nursery Cryme, Foxtrot, Selling England by the Pound* and *The Lamb Lies Down On Broadway*. As with the other two box sets, a DVD accompanied each of the albums with a 5.1 surround sound mix together with interviews, live performances and reproduced tour programs.

One additional CD and DVD pair included extra tracks, made up of singles and B-sides not available on the original albums, with the bulk of the CD comprising the three tracks recorded for a BBC radio show in 1970 and the four tracks commissioned for the BBC documentary about Michael Jackson, the painter. All had previously been issued as part of the Genesis Archive 1967-1975 compilation with the main tracks of note being 'Frustration' that would become 'Anyway' on The Lamb Lies Down On Broadway, and 'Manipulation' which would morph into 'The Musical Box' on Nursery Cryme.

Genesis Live 1973-2007 (2009)

The last of the major box set releases with remixed tracks, this set focuses on the live recordings, with the exception of the *Live Over Europe 2007* release from two years earlier, although there were spaces allocated in the box set packaging to insert the *Live Over Europe 2007* CDs. This box set included the remixed versions of *Genesis Live, Seconds Out, Three Sides Live* and both the longs and shorts volumes of *The Way We Walk*. *Genesis Live* includes the extended content previously released in 2007 with a selection of live tracks from *The Lamb Lies Down On Broadway* recorded in Los Angeles in 1975. Rather than simply reproduce the two original CDs from the tour, the track order was modified to match the tour set list with the three older recordings of 'Mama', That's All' and 'In Too Deep' moved to the end of the second CD. A DVD accompanied each of the albums with a 5.1 surround sound mix of the album together with – once again – interviews and reproduced tour programs.

Additional, previously unreleased live recordings were added to the box set, including live material recorded in 1975 from the *Lamb Lies Down On Broadway* tour and a recording from the Rainbow in 1973 that includes 'Supper's Ready'.

R-Kive (2014)

Released to coincide with the BBC documentary *Genesis: Together and Apart*, which aired on 4 October 2014, the broadcast version was extended for a subsequent DVD release, *Genesis: Sum of the Parts*. The album has a selection of Genesis tracks from every album except *From Genesis To Revelation* and individual solo tracks from Banks, Collins, Gabriel, Hackett and Rutherford. The tracks are presented in a chronology from 1970 through to 2012. It does, however, fail to include any tracks from the sixteen solo album releases by Anthony Phillips.

Compilations
Turn It On Again – Best of '81-83' (1991)
Recorded at various studios and live venues

The first of three releases to use this name, this compilation covers the studio albums *Abacab* and *Genesis* plus the EP from the *Abacab* sessions *3x3* and the live album *Three Sides Live*. Although the title suggests that it covers 1981 to 1983 and all the tracks were recorded during this period, it includes live versions of songs from 1973's *Selling England By The Pound*, 1978's *...and then there were three...* and 1980's *Duke*. The compilation is a record of how much the band had morphed into a chart-topping rock and pop band before *Invisible Touch* in 1986, and it does work well as a catch-up for those newer fans who had started to follow the band with *Invisible Touch* and its string of five top five hits. The cover was designed by Studio R+M and is a simple affair with a picture of the three main band members.

A couple of tracks are worth a mention here, as they only appear on this first version of the compilations:
'Turn It on Again (live)' 9:03 (Banks, Collins, Rutherford)
This song was recorded at the same time as the other material for the 1982 album *Three Sides Live*, but not included on that release. The track also includes a medley of four other songs, 'Everybody Needs Somebody' from the Blues Brothers, 'Satisfaction / The Last Time' from the Rolling Stones, 'All Day And All Of The Night' from The Kinks and 'The Midnight Hour' from Wilson Pickett. The Blues Brothers medley used on the 1980 tour was later dropped as it was thought a bad idea – a bit too much Collins in spirit and not very Genesis.
'Firth Of Fifth (live)' 9:22 (Genesis)
Recorded at the same time as the other material for the 1982 album *Three Sides Live*, but not included in the release. This is a complete oddball as it was released in 1973 and was the only track on the album not to have been a single.

Turn It On Again – The Hits (1999)
A new, updated version of the '81-83' compilation was released in 1999 adding additional hits from *Invisible Touch,* and *We Can't Dance*. 'Firth Of Fifth' is replaced by the hit single from *Selling England By The Pound*, 'I Know What I Like (In Your Wardrobe)'. The album now covered the years 1973 to 1999 while 'The Carpet Crawlers 1999' brought things up to date, the most recent offering elsewhere being the last single from the *We Can't dance* album in 1991.

The album cover was designed by Wherefore Art? and has yet another Genesis logo made up from letters taken from the previous logos, making a great trivia question for Genesis fans. The G is from *...and then there were three...*, the E from the second E on *We Can't Dance*, the N from *Calling All Stations*, the E from *The Lamb Lies Down On Broadway*, the S from *Duke*, the I from *Genesis* and finally the S from *Invisible Touch*.

Turn It On Again – The Hits – The Tour Edition (2007)
To coincide with the 2007 tour, Virgin chose to use this name for the third time to release a different selection of studio recordings, remastered in 2007. The compilation is increased to a double CD with the addition of more singles. Despite the 'Tour Edition' part of the title, none of this was recorded live on the 2007 tour; it was just another way to jump on the tour publicity and sell some more units. The sleeve design was by again by Chris Peyton, using both the new composite logo from the previous *The Hits* version of the compilation and the characters referencing the six albums from the *Platinum Collection*.

50 Years Ago (2017)
Recorded at Regent Sound studio in London in August 1968

Released as a digital download only, this album contains the tracks from the first album *From Genesis To Revelation* but also has additional material that was discovered in storage at Regent studios, where the original recordings were made. Released by Jonathan King on his own JonJo label, there are several new mixes included, although the constraints a four-track recording offers limited mixing opportunities. The most notable are tracks such as 'Fireside Song', 'Silent Sun' and 'Where The Sweet Turns To Sour' which have the overbearing strings removed – though to do this they only had to mute tracks three and four on the master which were used for strings and brass. Other tracks have the brass reduced in volume, but not removed. The release acts as an opportunity to hear how some of the early recordings would have sounded as the band would have heard them in the studio before the orchestration was added to the tracks.

Video Releases

This section details the video releases that were either released directly to DVD, or have been converted to DVD from videotape, and are still available. There are numerous low budget releases, many of which are also low quality, with interview clips or concert footage, many were only available on the various videotape formats and have not been included here, although most of these are still available on YouTube.

Genesis: In Concert (1976)

Recorded at: The Apollo Theatre, Glasgow, Scotland on 9 July 1976 and Bingley
Running time: 45:00

Recorded live at two gigs on the *Trick of the Tail* tour in 1976 and released on videotape, this video includes a short segment over the titles showing part of the gear load-in and a portion of the setup with 'I Know What I Like (In Your Wardrobe)' as the musical backing. The contents of this video were included as an extra DVD with the 2007 remix release of *A Trick of the Tail* CD. I was at the Glasgow Apollo gig – the second of two nights – and I remember the sheer noise of the crowd, which was like the roar of a football crowd, which really comes across on the recording. There isn't any information on which songs were recorded where, but I can tell that sections filmed from the stage during 'Supper's Ready' were Glasgow, as you can see the huge drop from the stage to the audience. The fall was 15 foot 6 inches but looked higher when viewed from the stalls, and indeed much higher when viewed from the edge of the stage. Health and safety hadn't gone nuts yet in 1976, thankfully. The clip of the audience at the end of 'Supper's Ready' is taken from the Bingley Hall concert, as you can see how low the stage was, indeed most of the long shots from behind the audience seem to have been taken from that concert. It is a pity that so much was cut out and specifically, that didn't include all of 'Supper's Ready' at least. According to the producer Tony Malam, the complete footage of both concerts, from all camera angles still exists in a vault somewhere.

Three Sides Live (1982)

Recorded at: Nassau Coliseum, Uniondale, New York on 29 November 1981, Savoy Theatre New York on 28 November 1981 and Birmingham NEC, England on 23 December 1981
Running time: 131 minutes

Released to coincide with the double album of the same name, this video is a documentary rather than a concert video, featuring live recordings from the shows at Nassau Coliseum, New York and the Savoy Theatre, New York from November 1981, mixed with interviews and behind the scenes video. As such, it becomes frustrating at times as many of the songs are only partially presented, and the footage often cuts away to band member comments or other footage of the tour. Aside from the shortcomings of the presentation format, it provides a real insight into the band and the challenges of a major tour, with access not normally possible unless you were a crew member at the time. Much of the material is taken from *Abacab* and *Duke* except for the seventies medley, and 'Afterglow,' while several full-length audio-only tracks are included. As with most of the other video releases, this was remastered and remixed in 5.1 surround sound by Nick Davis for the November 2009 release *Genesis Movie Box 1981 – 2007* DVD box set. The original 16mm film made at the time was later restored and given an updated, higher resolution polish for a BluRay release in 2014.

The Mama Tour (1985)
Recorded at: NEC Birmingham, England, February 1984
Running time: 131 minutes

This video was filmed between 25 and 29 February 1984 at the National Exhibition Centre, Birmingham, UK where the band played five nights at this large, 16,000 seats indoor arena. It was the only venue for the European leg of the *Mama* tour promoting the *Genesis* album. Highlights are the ever-present seventies medley, this version including sections of 'In The Cage', 'Cinema Show', '…In That Quiet Earth', 'The Colony Of Slippermen' and 'Afterglow'. 'Turn It On Again' features another medley, with a string of hits from other artists including The Blues Brothers, The Rolling Stones, The Kinks and Wilson Pickett. Missing from the release is yet another medley from the live shows that included 'The Eleventh Earl Of Mar', 'The Lamb Lies Down On Broadway', 'Firth Of Fifth' and 'Cinema Show'. The contents were remastered and remixed in 5.1 surround sound by Nick Davis for the November 2009 release *Genesis Movie Box 1981 – 2007* DVD box set.

Visible Touch (1987)
Running time: 48 minutes plus documentary

This is a compilation of the music videos made for the five singles released from *Invisible Touch* plus the video for 'Anything She Does' starring Benny Hill which was used at the start of the gigs on that tour. All five singles reached the top five in the US charts. They were 'Throwing It All Away', 'Tonight, Tonight, Tonight', 'Land Of Confusion', 'In Too Deep' and 'Invisible Touch'. A short tour documentary is also included. The contents would be included in *The Video Show* DVD released in 2004 with other video clips from later albums, and the tour video would form part of the *Live At Wembley Stadium* DVD.

Invisible Touch Tour (1988)
Recorded at: Wembley Stadium, London, on 1 to 4 July 1987.
Running time: 115 minutes

This video was filmed at Wembley Stadium, in July 1987 where the band ended their world tour with four shows in front of 288,000 fans. This iconic venue had hosted *Live Aid* two years earlier. This video would later be re-released in 2003 on DVD as *Live At Wembley Stadium* with the addition of a tour documentary.

The 'Turn It On Again Medley' includes short sections of 'Everybody Needs Somebody to Love', '(I Can't Get No) Satisfaction', 'Twist and Shout', 'Reach Out (I'll Be There)', 'You've Lost That Lovin' Feelin'', 'Pinball Wizard', 'In the Midnight Hour', 'Turn It On Again (Reprise)'.

'Do The Neurotic' is included, but only as part of the video credits.

Genesis Live – The Way We Walk – In Concert (1993)
Recorded at: Earls Court, London, England on 8 November 1992
Running time: 139 minutes (DVD version)

This live concert video was recorded at Earls Court, London on 8 November 1992 on the We *Can't Dance* tour and provides the video companion to the CD releases *The Way We Walk Vol 1 – The Shorts* and *The Way We Walk Vol 2 – The Longs*. Initially released on VHS Video and Laserdisc, the content was reissued in 2002 as *The Way We Walk – Live in Concert*, and further remastered and remixed in 5.1 surround sound by Nick Davis for the November 2009 release *Genesis Movie Box 1981 – 2007* DVD box set. The 2002 DVD version added extra material, including interviews with Collins, Rutherford and Banks, plus a commentary audio track. Options were also included to allow viewing the DVD from one of the four camera angles used in the production as well as tour images and a reproduction of the original tour programme.

The concert captures one of the better tours in the later part of the band's career. The choice of material and its execution were amongst the most pleasing, including the exceptional twenty minutes 'Old Medley', a highlight that had been growing and improving with each tour. Unfortunately, this was a period where the range of Collins' voice was starting to become limited, and many of the songs were transposed to lower keys to accommodate this. The only slight disappointment in terms of the set listing is that for some reason only the second half of 'Driving The Last Spike' was included on any of the versions released. This cannot have been for space reasons but was most likely an issue with either the performance or sound quality of the first half of the song.

The Genesis Songbook (2001)
Running time: 100 minutes

This DVD is a great history of the band with a collection of interviews covering key points in their journey as well as discussions on many of the band's favourite songs. There are contributions from most of the past band members including Gabriel, Hackett, original member Anthony Phillips and John Silver who played the drums on the first album. The film covers the entire history as far as *Calling All Stations* and includes interviews with Ray Wilson plus their manager Tony Smith, journalist Chris Welch, producer David Hentschel and many others. The video has some clips of Collins, Banks and Rutherford playing simple versions of some of their better-known songs.

Genesis Live at Wembley Stadium (2003)
Recorded at: Wembley Stadium London, 1 to 4 July 1987
Running time: 115 minutes concert plus extras

Reissue of 1989 Invisible Touch tour video filmed at Wembley Stadium in July 1987 at the end of the world tour with the tour documentary added.

When in Rome 2007 (2008)
Recorded at: Circus Maximus, Rome, Italy on 14 July 2007
Running time: 5:42:00 (157 minutes are the actual concert)

A three DVD set, two of which cover the free concert at the Circus Maximus in Rome on 14 July 2007 at the end of the European leg of the *Turn It On Again: The Tour*. The third DVD is a documentary *Come Rain Or Shine* filmed during the tour with extensive behind the scenes footage.

Genesis The Movie Box (2009)
Recorded at: various locations between 1981 – 2007
Running time: 9:33:16

A compilation box set of four concert footage videos from 1981 – 1992 including *Three Sides Live*, *The Mama Tour*, *Live At Wembley Stadium* and *The Way We Walk – Live In Concert*. *When In Rome* was not included but an empty jewel case was provided to add the three DVDs to the set. An additional new DVD *Behind The Music* from a VH1 special was also included, which is a good historical synopsis of the band with contributions for almost everyone who played with Genesis between 1966 and 2007.

Bibliography
Books
Bowler D., Dray B., *Genesis: A Biography* (Sidgwick & Jackson, 1992)
Rutherford M., *The Living Years, the first Genesis memoir* (Constable, 2014)
Collins P., *Not Dead Yet: The Autobiography* (Arrow, 2017)
Banks T., Collins P., Gabriel P., Hackett S., Rutherford M., *Chapter & Verse* (Weidenfeld & Nicholson, 2007)
MacPhail R. with Charlesworth C., *My Book Of Genesis* (Argyle & Bute 2017)

Videos
Genesis – In their own words (Granada TV 1980)
The Genesis Songbook (Eagle Rock, 2008)
Genesis – The Gabriel Era (Classic Rock Legends 2006)

Online Resources
www.genesis-news.com
www.tabletopgenesis.com
www.genesisarchive.com

Would you like to write for Sonicbond Publishing?

At Sonicbond Publishing we are always on the look-out for authors, particularly for our two main series:

On Track. Mixing fact with in depth analysis, the On Track series examines the work of a particular musical artist or group. All genres are considered from easy listening and jazz to 60s soul to 90s pop, via rock and metal.

On Screen. This series looks at the world of film and television. Subjects considered include directors, actors and writers, as well as entire television and film series. As with the On Track series, we balance fact with analysis.

While professional writing experience would, of course, be an advantage the most important qualification is to have real enthusiasm and knowledge of your subject. First-time authors are welcomed, but the ability to write well in English is essential.

Sonicbond Publishing has distribution throughout Europe and North America, and all books are also published in E-book form. Authors will be paid a royalty based on sales of their book.

Further details are available from www.sonicbondpublishing.co.uk. To contact us, complete the contact form there or

email info@sonicbondpublishing.co.uk

Also from Sonicbond Publishing

On Track series
Queen Andrew Wild 978-1-78952-003-3
Emerson Lake and Palmer Mike Goode 978-1-78952-000-2
Deep Purple and Rainbow 1968-79 Steve Pilkington 978-1-78952-002-6
Yes Stephen Lambe 978-1-78952-001-9
Blue Oyster Cult Jacob Holm-Lupo 978-1-78952-007-1
The Beatles Andrew Wild 978-1-78952-009-5
Roy Wood and the Move James R Turner 978-1-78952-008-8
Genesis Stuart MacFarlane 978-1-78952-005-7
Jethro Tull Jordan Blum 978-1-78952-016-3
The Rolling Stones 1963-80 Steve Pilkington 978-1-78952-017-0
Judas Priest John Tucker 978-1-78952-018-7
Toto Jacob Holm-Lupo 978-1-78952-019-4
Van Der Graaf Generator Dan Coffey 978-1-78952-031-6
Frank Zappa 1966 to 1979 Eric Benac 978-1-78952-033-0
Elton John in the 1970s Peter Kearns 978-1-78952-034-7
The Moody Blues Geoffrey Feakes 978-1-78952-042-2
The Beatles Solo 1969-1980 Andrew Wild 978-1-78952-042-2
Steely Dan Jez Rowden 978-1-78952-043-9

On Screen series
Carry On... Stephen Lambe 978-1-78952-004-0
Audrey Hepburn Ellen Cheshire 978-1-78952-011-8
Powell and Pressburger Sam Proctor 978-1-78952-013-2
Seinfeld Seasons 1 to 5 Stephen Lambe 978-1-78952-012-5
Francis Ford Coppola Stephen Lambe 978-1-78952-022-4

Other Books
Not As Good As The Book Andy Tillison 978-1-78952-021-7
The Voice. Frank Sinatra in the 1940s
Stephen Lambe 978-1-78952-032-3

and many more to come!